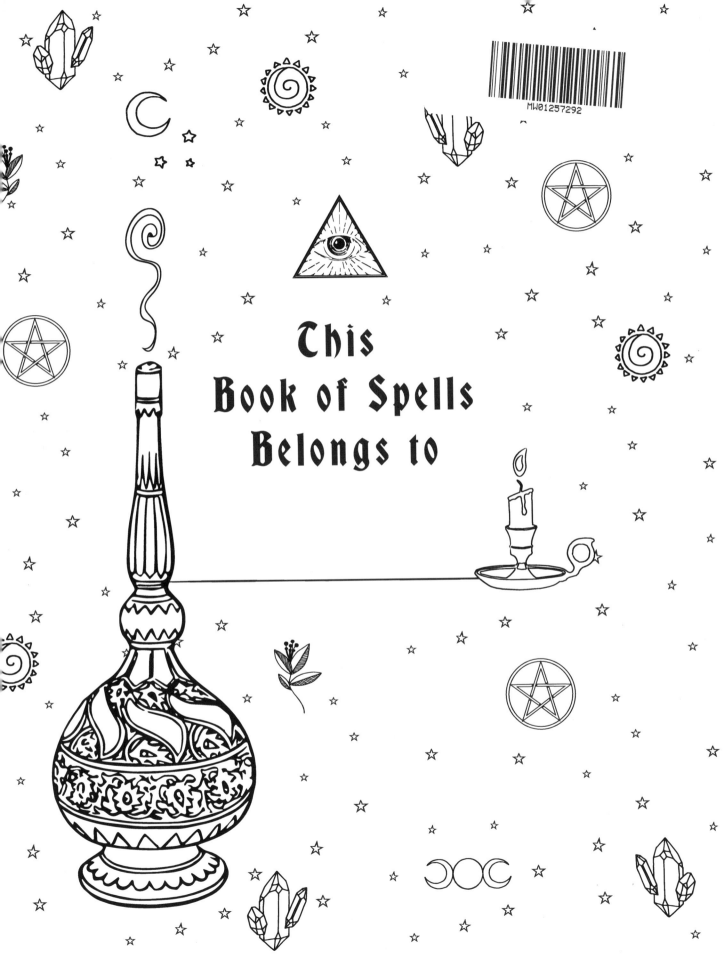

This
Book of Spells
Belongs to

An' it harm none, do what ye will

Wheel of the Year

Yule
DEC 21

Samhain
OCT 31

Imbolc
FEB 2

sagittarius
capricorn
scorpio
aquarius

Mabon
SEP 21

Ostara
MAR 21

libra
pisces
virgo
aries

Lammas
AUG 1

Beltane
MAY 1

leo
taurus
cancer
gemini

Litha
JUNE 21

Lunar Calendar

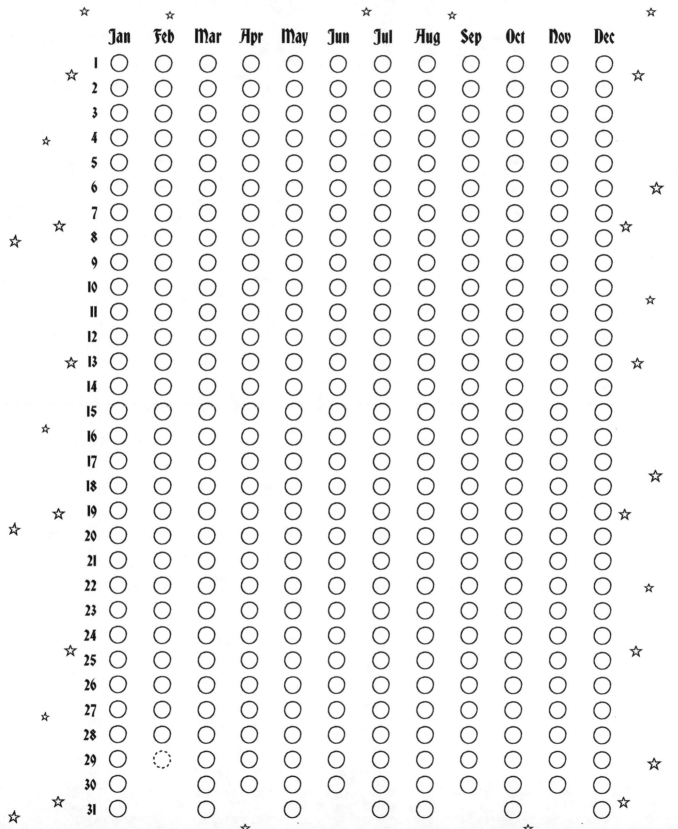

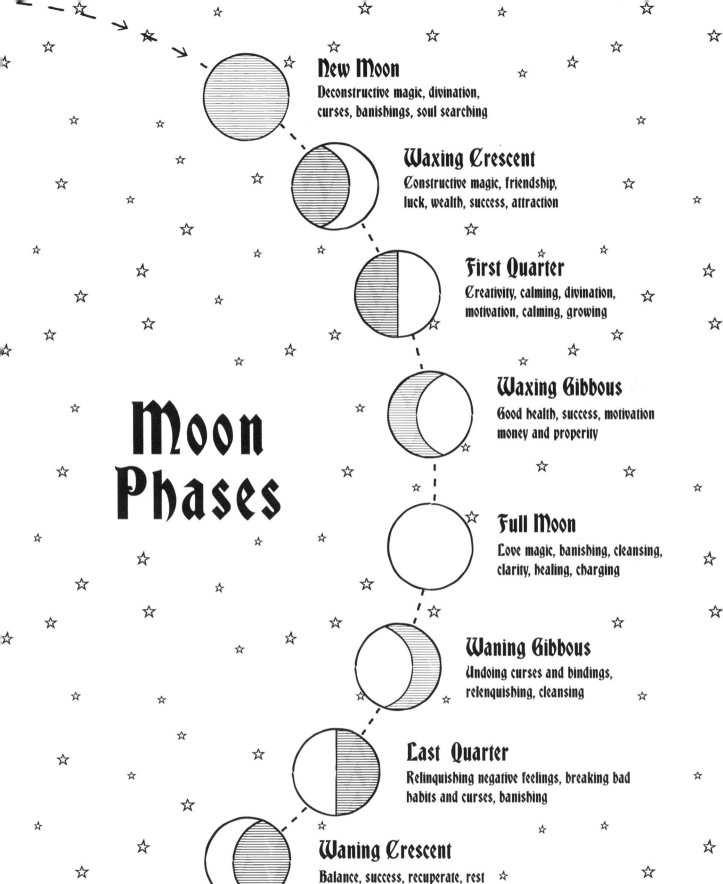

New Moon
Deconstructive magic, divination, curses, banishings, soul searching

Waxing Crescent
Constructive magic, friendship, luck, wealth, success, attraction

First Quarter
Creativity, calming, divination, motivation, calming, growing

Waxing Gibbous
Good health, success, motivation money and properity

Full Moon
Love magic, banishing, cleansing, clarity, healing, charging

Waning Gibbous
Undoing curses and bindings, relenquishing, cleansing

Last Quarter
Relinquishing negative feelings, breaking bad habits and curses, banishing

Waning Crescent
Balance, success, recuperate, rest attaining knowledge and wisdom

Moon Phases

Notes

Theban Script Alphabet

Table of Contents

Ritual	Type	Page

Table of Contents

Ritual	Type	Page

Book of Spells

Notes

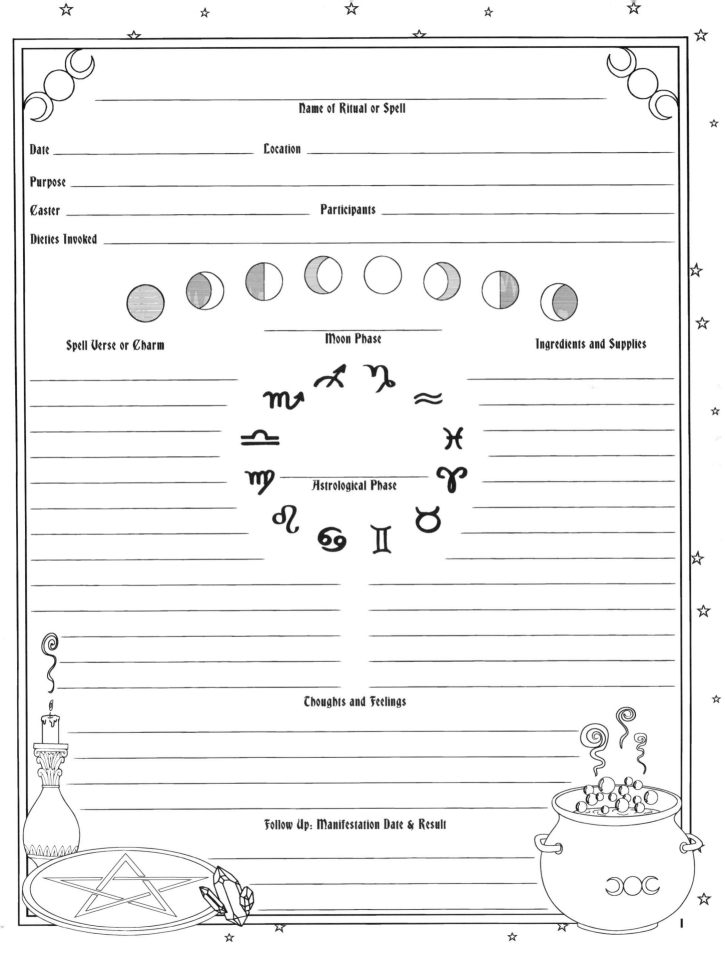

_____
Name of Ritual or Spell

Date _____ **Location** _____

Purpose _____

Caster _____ **Participants** _____

Dieties Invoked _____

Spell Verse or Charm **Moon Phase** **Ingredients and Supplies**

Astrological Phase

Thoughts and Feelings

Follow Up: Manifestation Date & Result

Notes

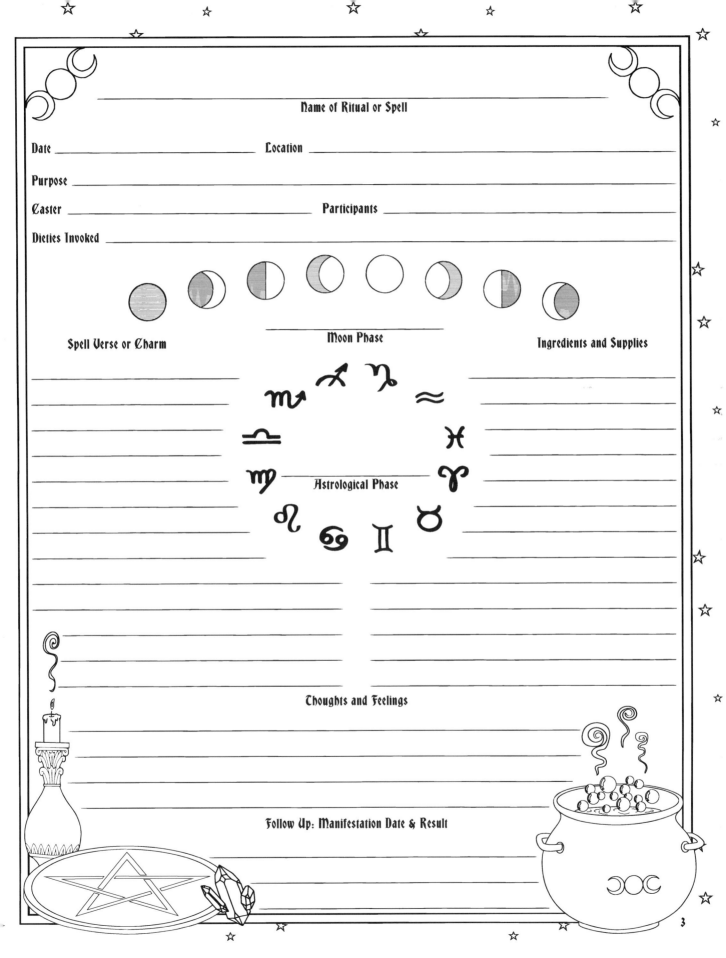

_____
Name of Ritual or Spell

Date _____ Location _____

Purpose _____

Caster _____ Participants _____

Dieties Invoked _____

Spell Verse or Charm   **Moon Phase**   **Ingredients and Supplies**

Astrological Phase

Thoughts and Feelings

Follow Up: Manifestation Date & Result

Notes

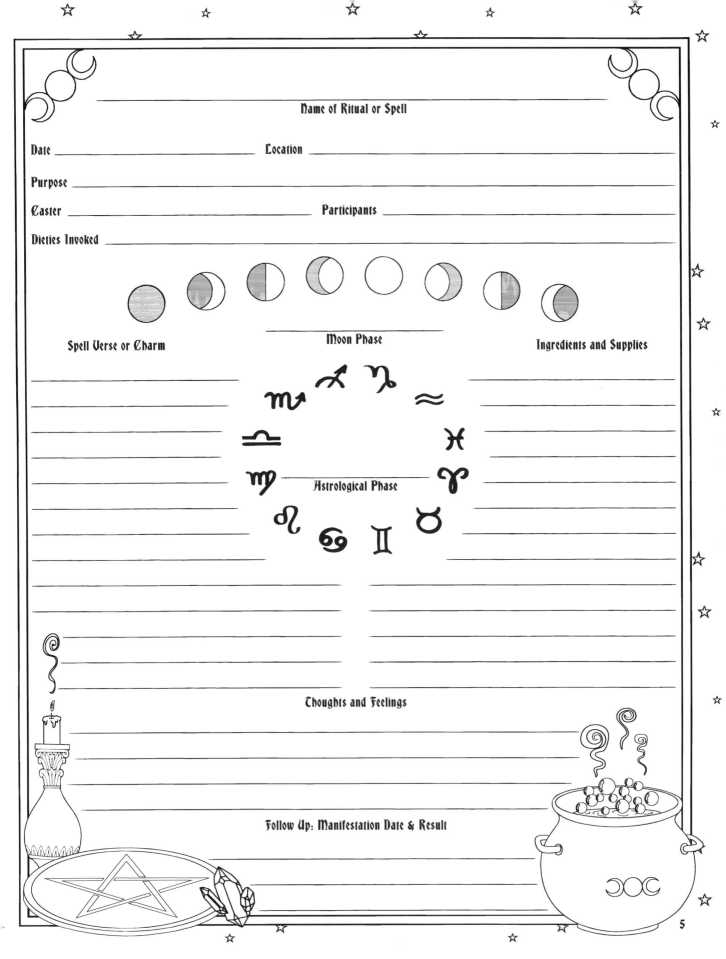

_____
Name of Ritual or Spell

Date _____ Location _____

Purpose _____

Caster _____ Participants _____

Dieties Invoked _____

Spell Verse or Charm   Moon Phase   Ingredients and Supplies

Astrological Phase

Thoughts and Feelings

Follow Up: Manifestation Date & Result

Notes

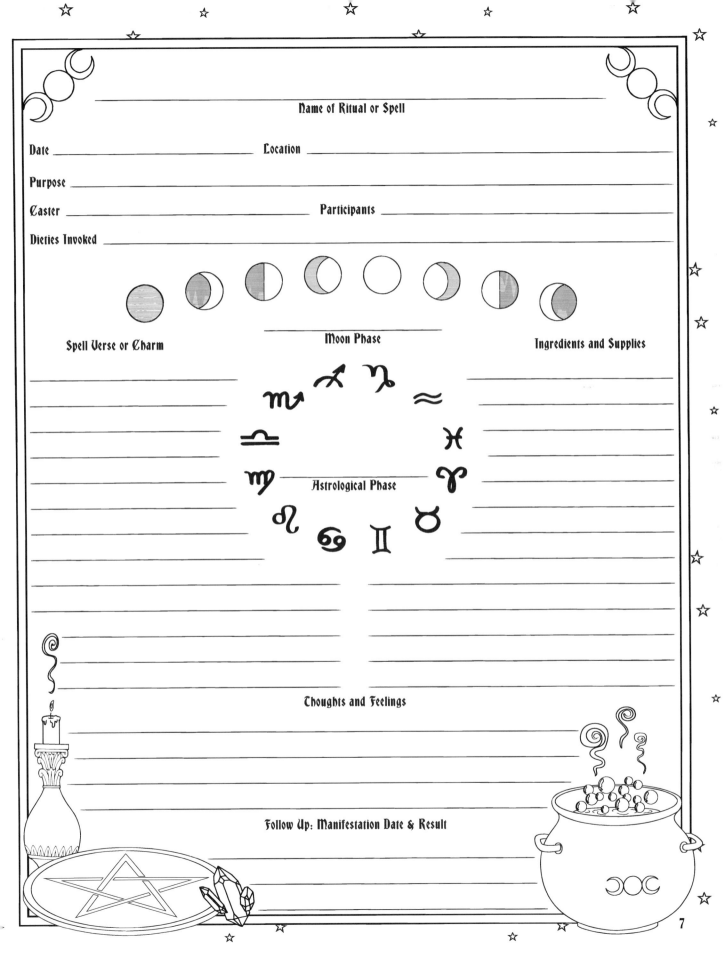

Name of Ritual or Spell

Date _____ Location _____

Purpose _____

Caster _____ Participants _____

Dieties Invoked _____

Spell Verse or Charm   **Moon Phase**   **Ingredients and Supplies**

Astrological Phase

Thoughts and Feelings

Follow Up: Manifestation Date & Result

Notes

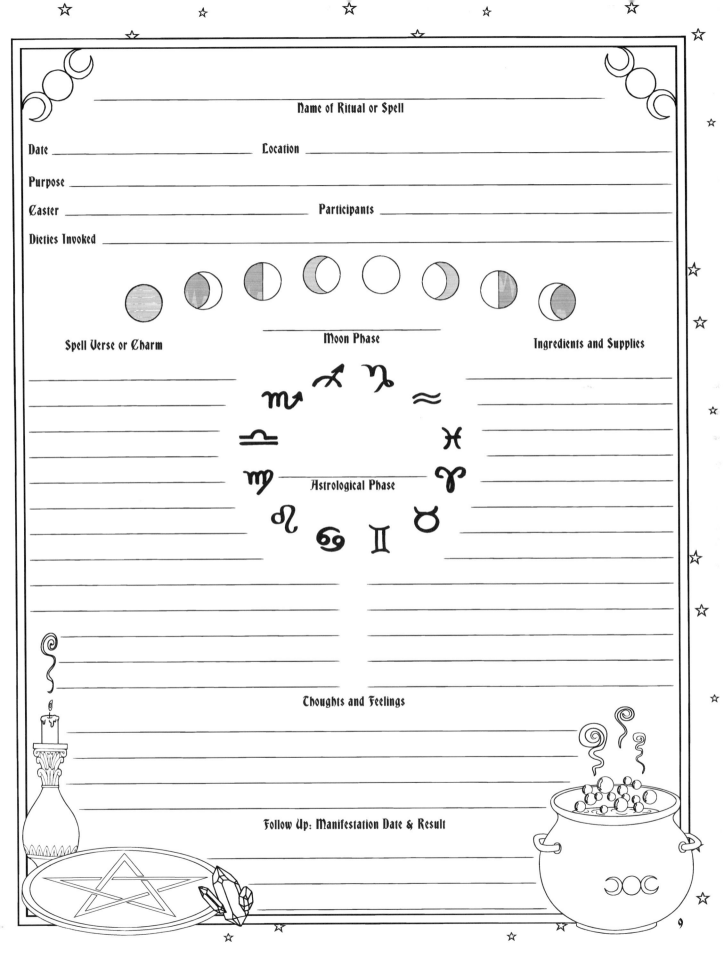

_____
Name of Ritual or Spell

Date _____   Location _____

Purpose _____

Caster _____   Participants _____

Dieties Invoked _____

Spell Verse or Charm   **Moon Phase**   **Ingredients and Supplies**

Astrological Phase

Thoughts and Feelings

Follow Up: Manifestation Date & Result

Notes

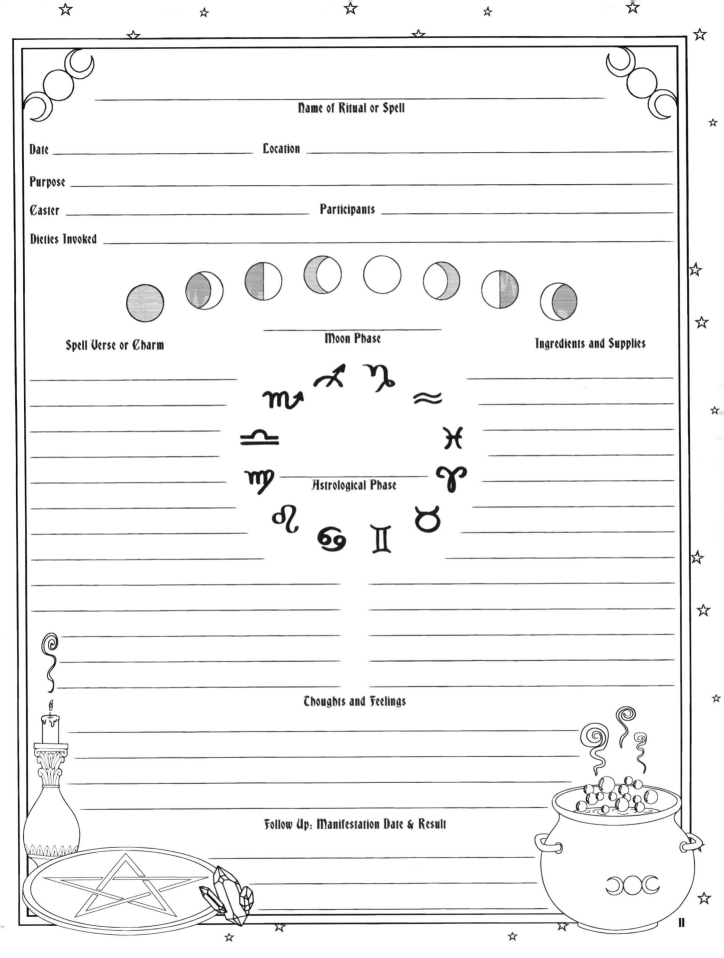

_____
Name of Ritual or Spell

Date _____   Location _____

Purpose _____

Caster _____   Participants _____

Dieties Invoked _____

Spell Verse or Charm   **Moon Phase**   **Ingredients and Supplies**

Astrological Phase

Thoughts and Feelings

Follow Up: Manifestation Date & Result

Notes

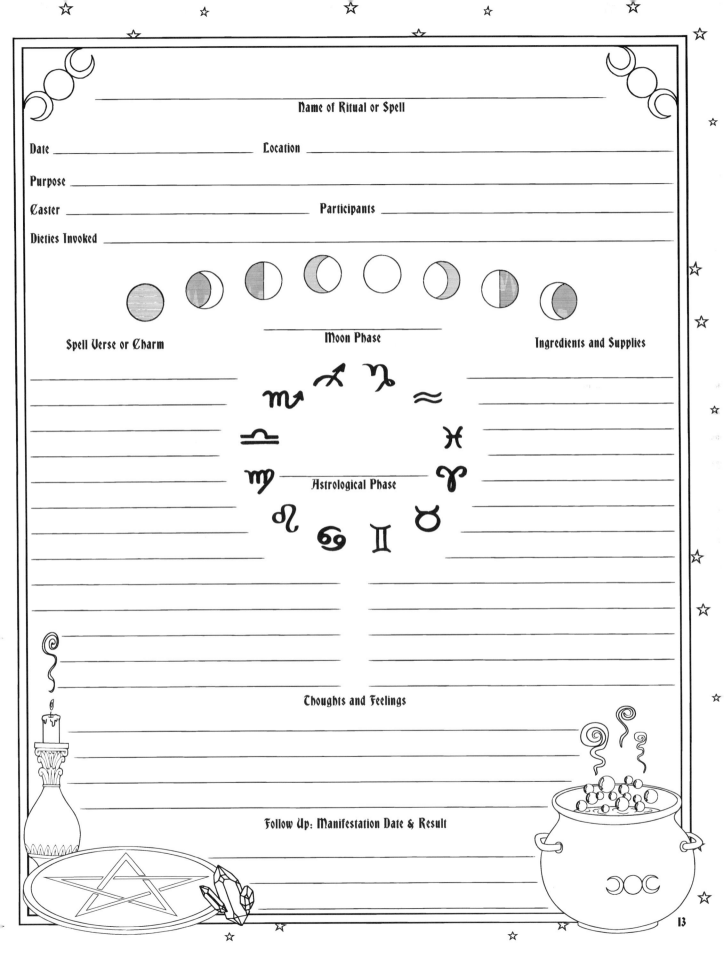

_____
Name of Ritual or Spell

Date _____   Location _____

Purpose _____

Caster _____   Participants _____

Dieties Invoked _____

Spell Verse or Charm   Moon Phase   Ingredients and Supplies

Astrological Phase

Thoughts and Feelings

Follow Up: Manifestation Date & Result

Notes

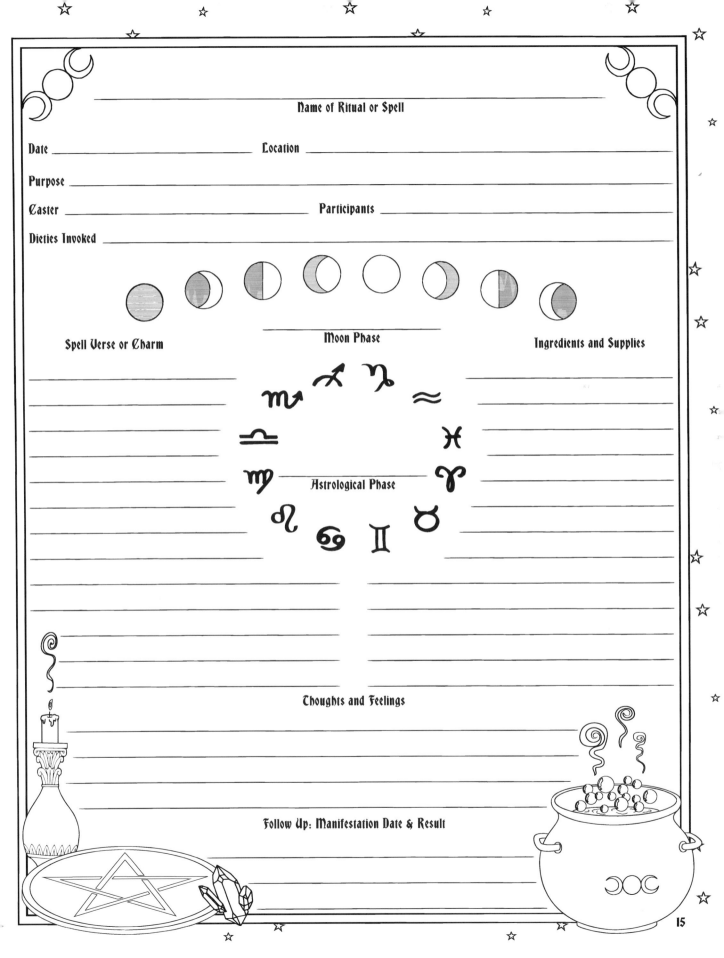

_____
Name of Ritual or Spell

Date _____ Location _____

Purpose _____

Caster _____ Participants _____

Dieties Invoked _____

Spell Verse or Charm   Moon Phase   Ingredients and Supplies

Astrological Phase

Thoughts and Feelings

Follow Up: Manifestation Date & Result

Notes

_____

Name of Ritual or Spell

Date _____ **Location** _____

Purpose _____

Caster _____ **Participants** _____

Dieties Invoked _____

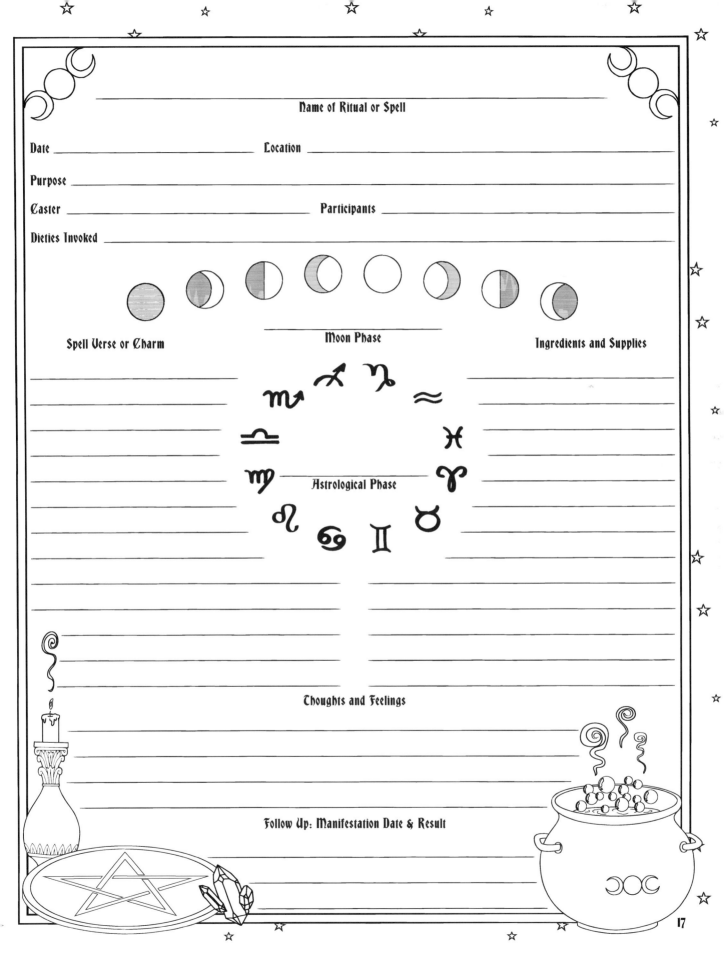

Spell Verse or Charm   **Moon Phase**   **Ingredients and Supplies**

Astrological Phase

Thoughts and Feelings

Follow Up: Manifestation Date & Result

Notes

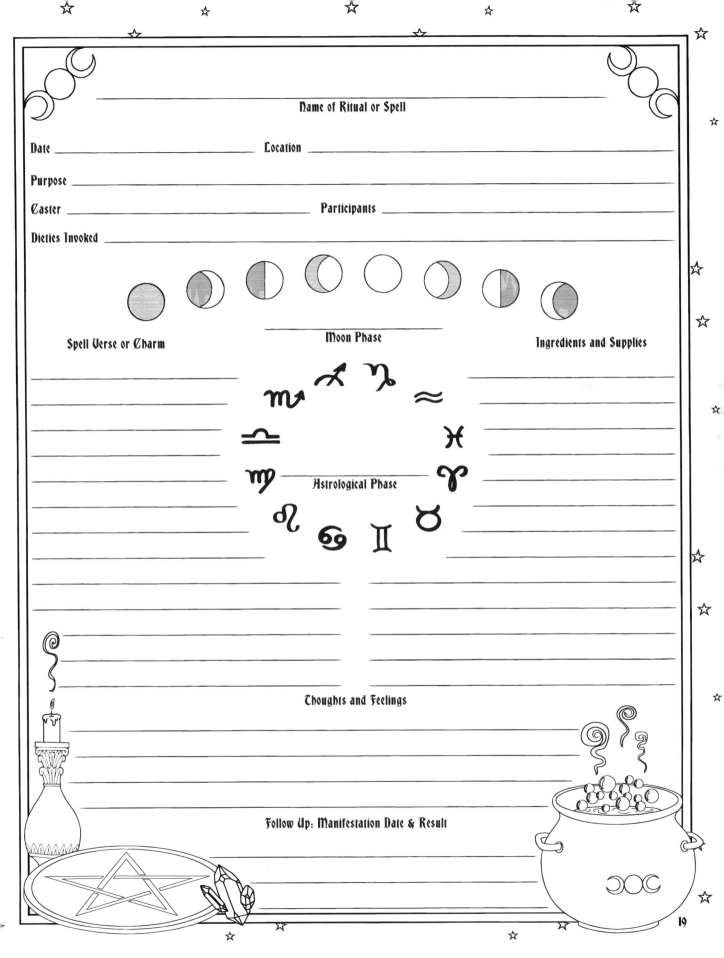

_____
Name of Ritual or Spell

Date _____ Location _____

Purpose _____

Caster _____ Participants _____

Dieties Invoked _____

Spell Verse or Charm   **Moon Phase**   **Ingredients and Supplies**

Astrological Phase

Thoughts and Feelings

Follow Up: Manifestation Date & Result

Notes

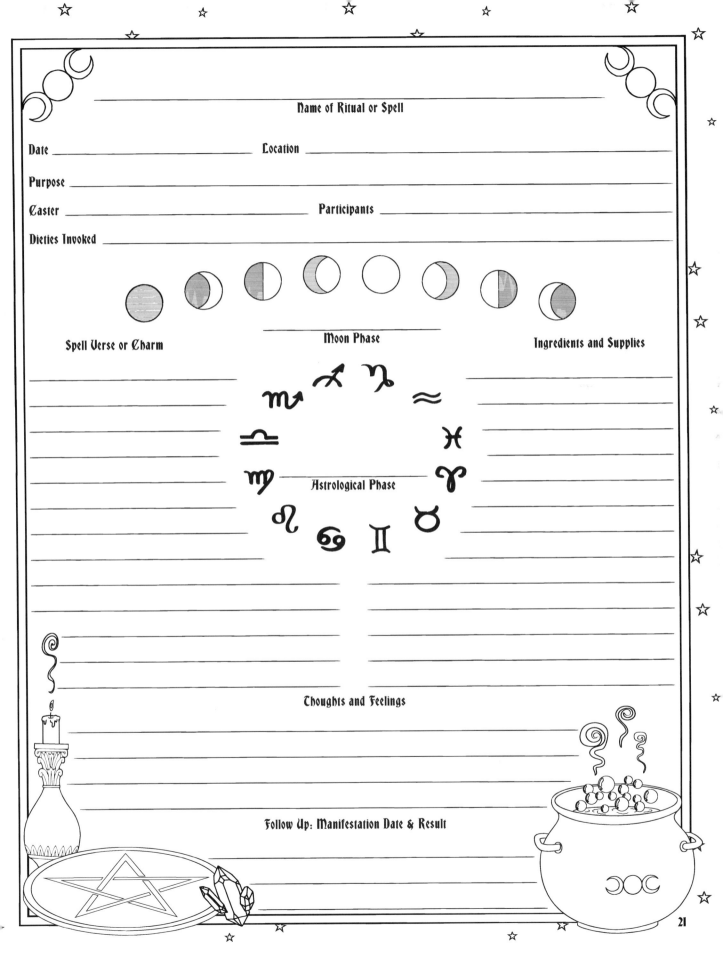

Name of Ritual or Spell

Date _____ Location _____

Purpose _____

Caster _____ Participants _____

Dieties Invoked _____

Spell Verse or Charm

Moon Phase

Ingredients and Supplies

Astrological Phase

Thoughts and Feelings

Follow Up: Manifestation Date & Result

Notes

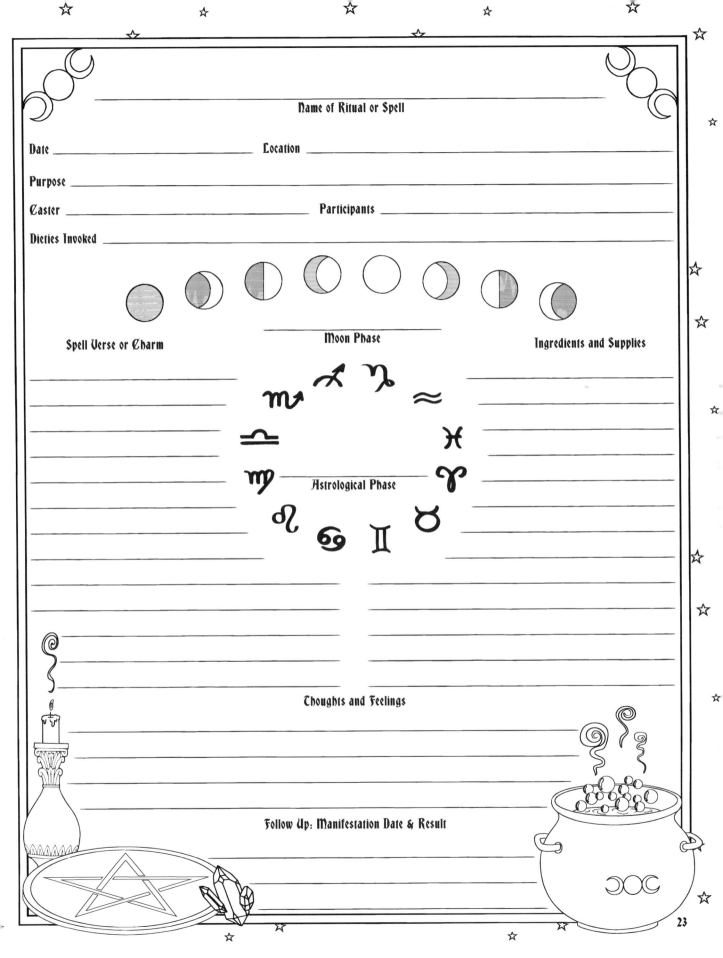

Name of Ritual or Spell

_____

Date _____ Location _____

Purpose _____

Caster _____ Participants _____

Dieties Invoked _____

Spell Verse or Charm   **Moon Phase**   **Ingredients and Supplies**

Astrological Phase

Thoughts and Feelings

Follow Up: Manifestation Date & Result

Notes

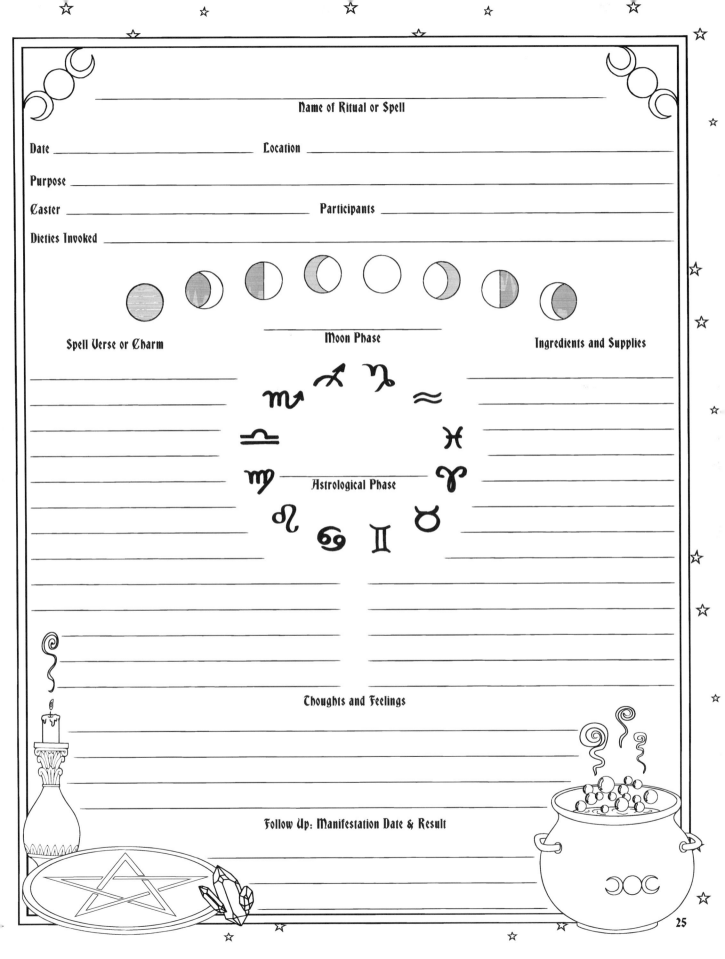

Name of Ritual or Spell

Date _____ Location _____

Purpose _____

Caster _____ Participants _____

Dieties Invoked _____

Spell Verse or Charm   Moon Phase   Ingredients and Supplies

Astrological Phase

Thoughts and Feelings

Follow Up: Manifestation Date & Result

Notes

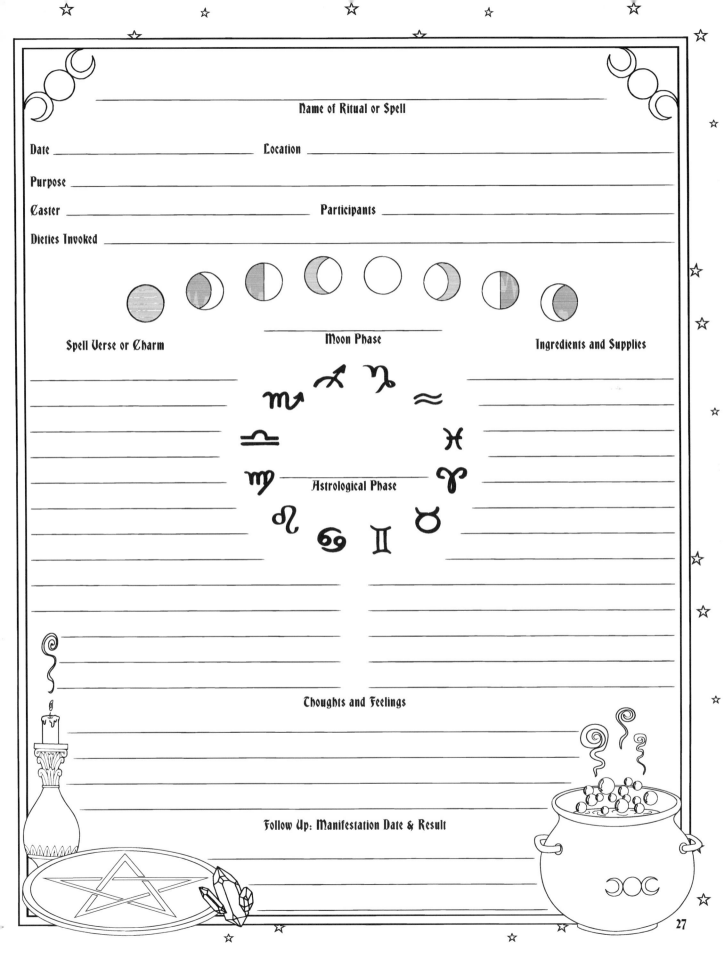

Name of Ritual or Spell

Date _____ Location _____

Purpose _____

Caster _____ Participants _____

Dieties Invoked _____

Spell Verse or Charm   **Moon Phase**   **Ingredients and Supplies**

Astrological Phase

Thoughts and Feelings

Follow Up: Manifestation Date & Result

Notes

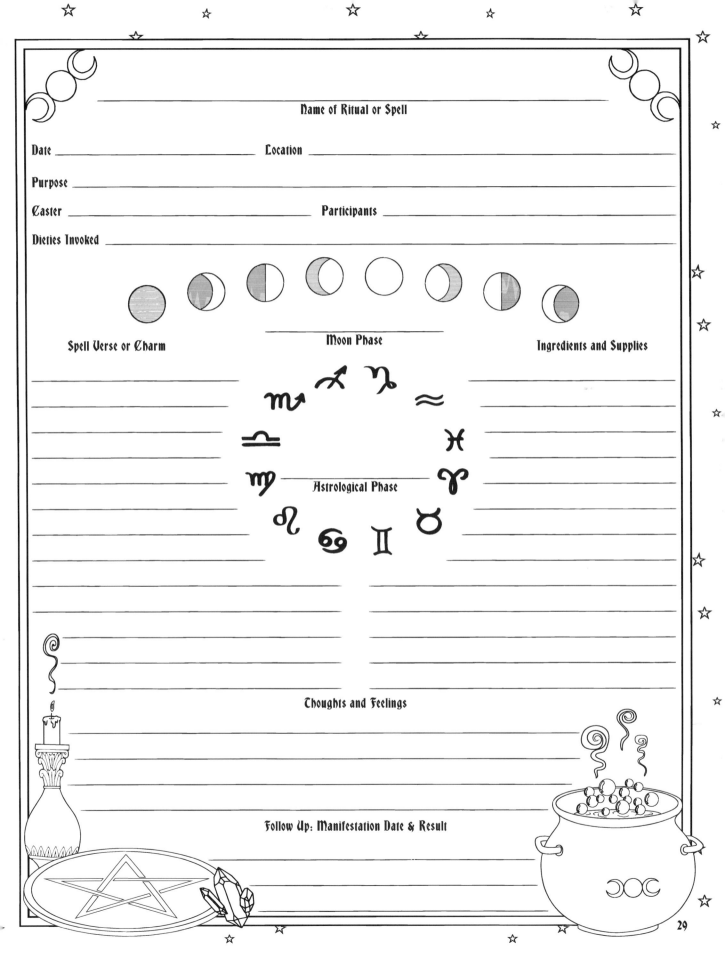

_____
Name of Ritual or Spell

Date _____   Location _____

Purpose _____

Caster _____   Participants _____

Dieties Invoked _____

Spell Verse or Charm   Moon Phase   Ingredients and Supplies

Astrological Phase

Thoughts and Feelings

Follow Up: Manifestation Date & Result

29

Notes

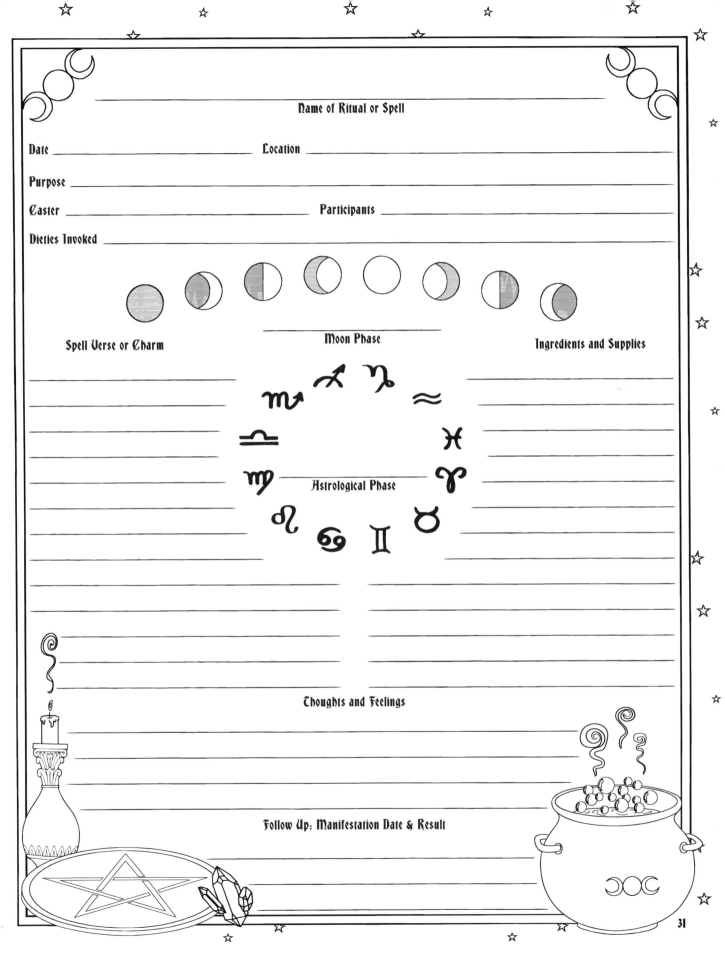

_____
Name of Ritual or Spell

Date _____ **Location** _____

Purpose _____

Caster _____ **Participants** _____

Dieties Invoked _____

Spell Verse or Charm   **Moon Phase**   **Ingredients and Supplies**

_____   _____

_____   _____

_____   _____

_____   **Astrological Phase**   _____

_____   _____

_____   _____

_____   _____

_____   _____

Thoughts and Feelings

_____

_____

Follow Up: Manifestation Date & Result

_____

Notes

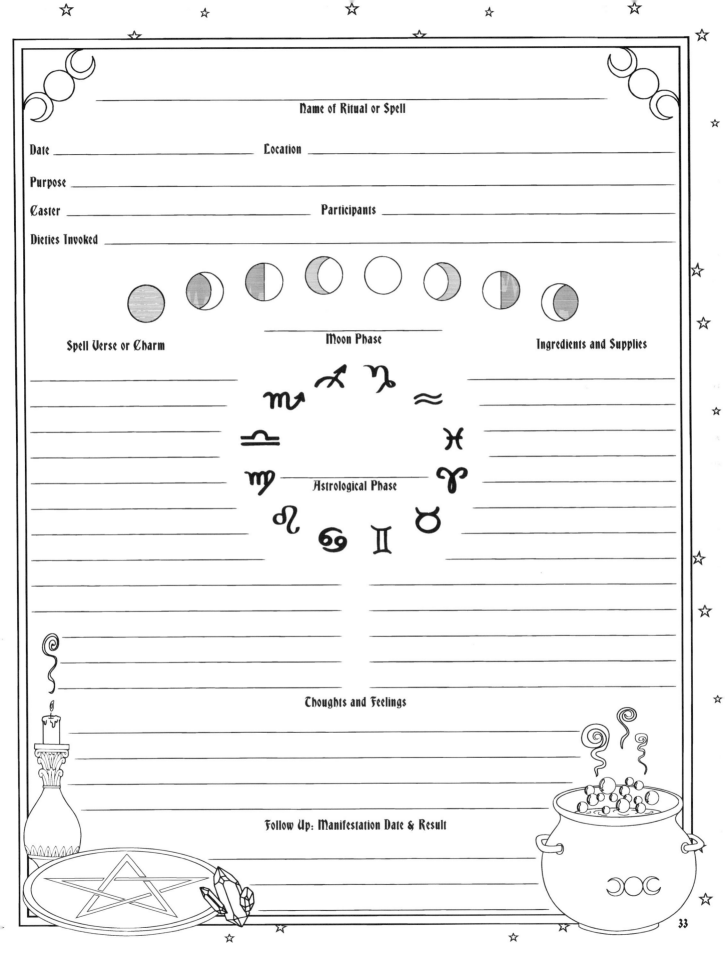

Name of Ritual or Spell

Date _____   Location _____

Purpose _____

Caster _____   Participants _____

Dieties Invoked _____

Spell Verse or Charm   Moon Phase   Ingredients and Supplies

Astrological Phase

Thoughts and Feelings

Follow Up: Manifestation Date & Result

Notes

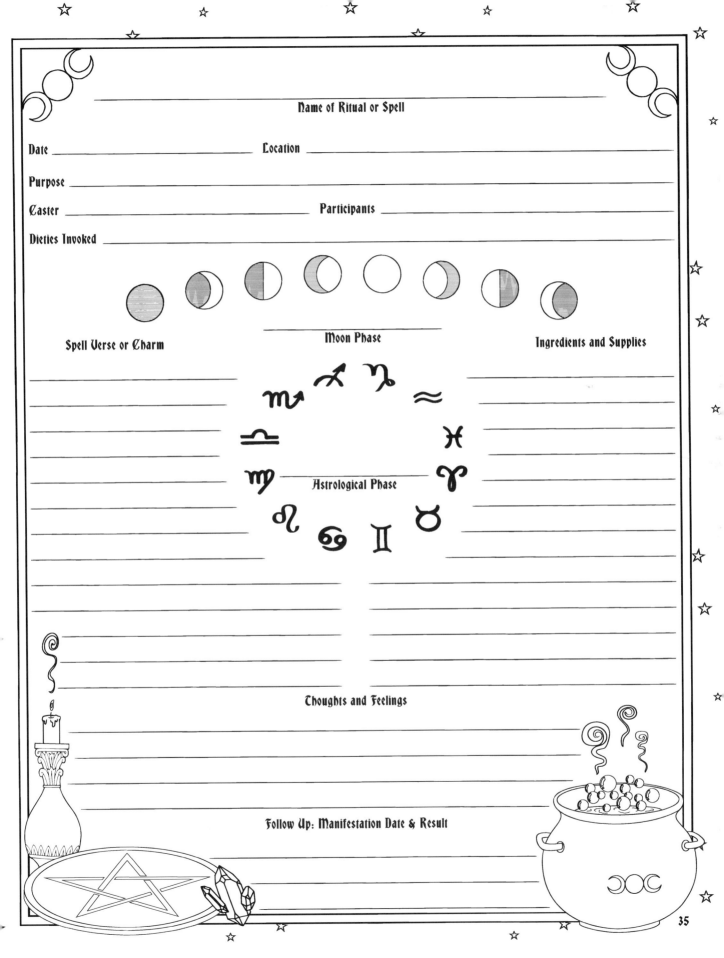

_____

Name of Ritual or Spell

Date _____ Location _____

Purpose _____

Caster _____ Participants _____

Dieties Invoked _____

Spell Verse or Charm   Moon Phase   Ingredients and Supplies

Astrological Phase

Thoughts and Feelings

Follow Up: Manifestation Date & Result

Notes

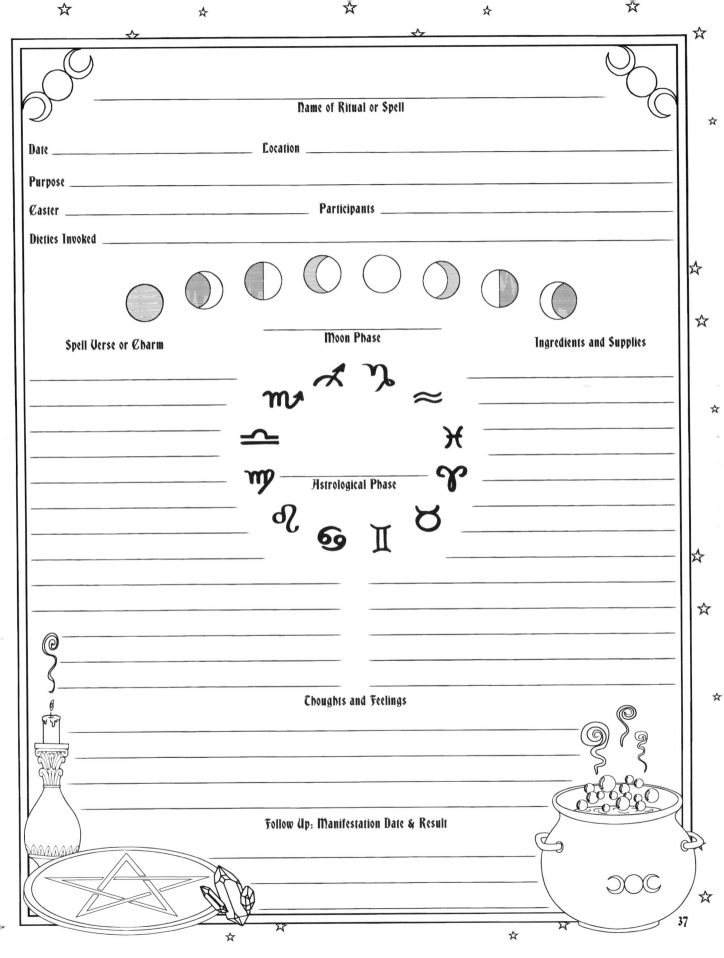

_____
Name of Ritual or Spell

Date _____ Location _____

Purpose _____

Caster _____ Participants _____

Dieties Invoked _____

Spell Verse or Charm   Moon Phase   Ingredients and Supplies

Astrological Phase

Thoughts and Feelings

Follow Up: Manifestation Date & Result

Notes

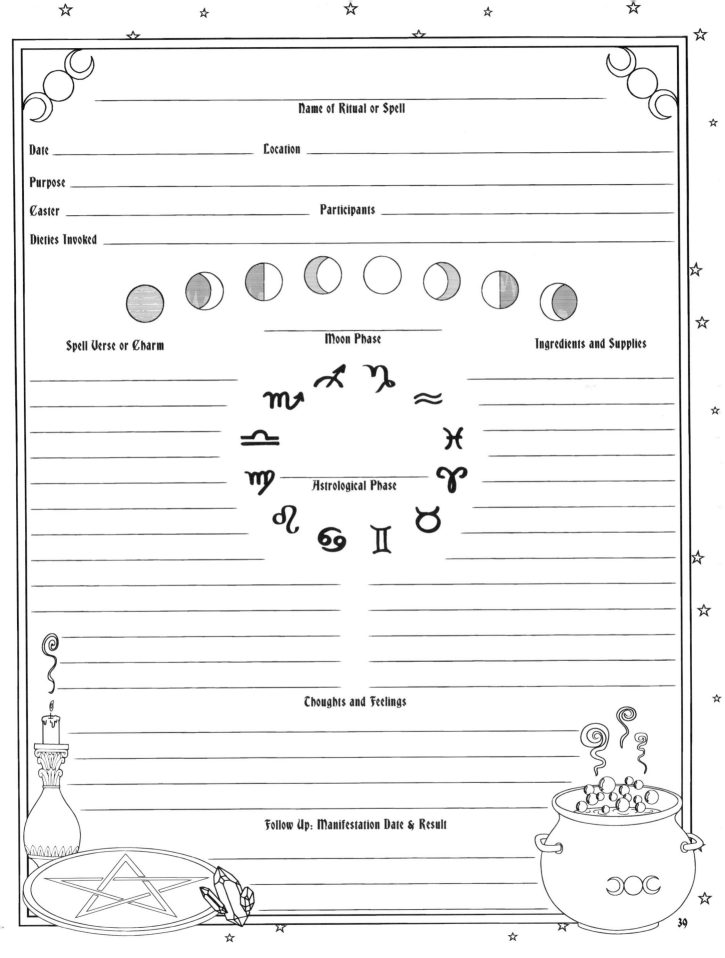

Name of Ritual or Spell

Date _____ Location _____

Purpose _____

Caster _____ Participants _____

Dieties Invoked _____

Spell Verse or Charm   Moon Phase   Ingredients and Supplies

Astrological Phase

Thoughts and Feelings

Follow Up: Manifestation Date & Result

Notes

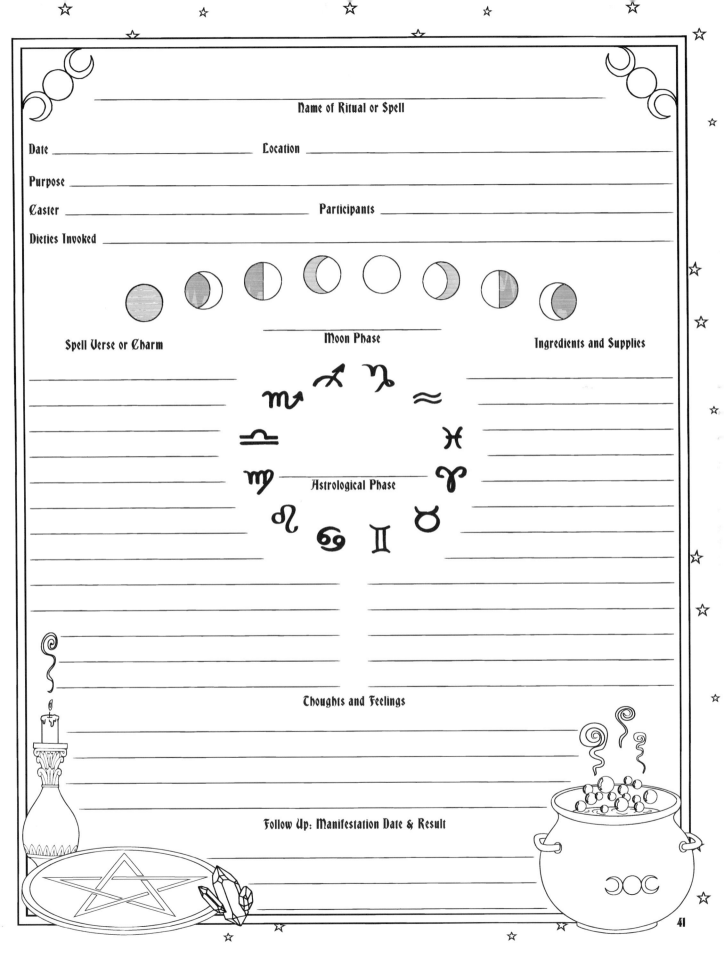

_____

Name of Ritual or Spell

Date _____ Location _____

Purpose _____

Caster _____ Participants _____

Dieties Invoked _____

Spell Verse or Charm   **Moon Phase**   **Ingredients and Supplies**

Astrological Phase

Thoughts and Feelings

Follow Up: Manifestation Date & Result

41

Notes

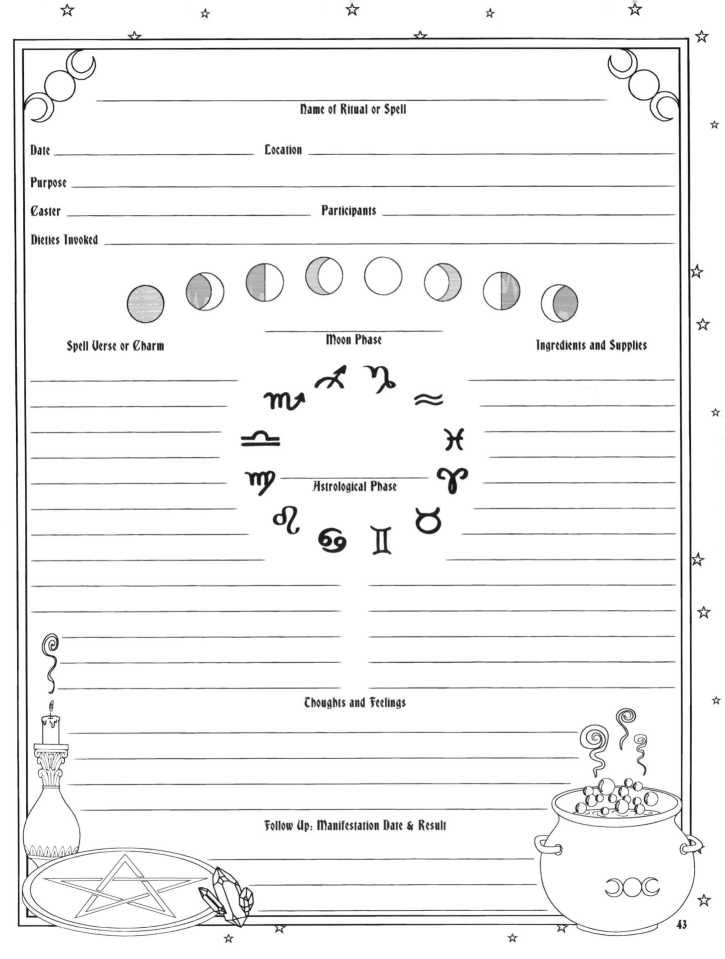

_____
Name of Ritual or Spell

Date _____   Location _____

Purpose _____

Caster _____   Participants _____

Dieties Invoked _____

Spell Verse or Charm   **Moon Phase**   **Ingredients and Supplies**

Astrological Phase

Thoughts and Feelings

Follow Up: Manifestation Date & Result

43

Notes

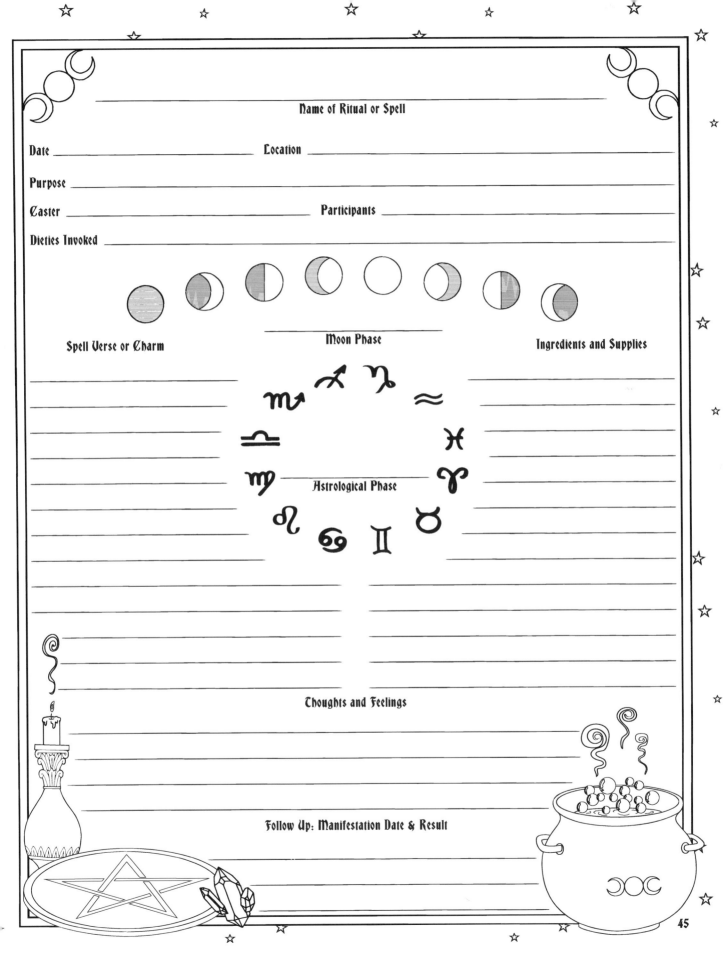

_____
Name of Ritual or Spell

Date _____ Location _____

Purpose _____

Caster _____ Participants _____

Dieties Invoked _____

Spell Verse or Charm   **Moon Phase**   **Ingredients and Supplies**

Astrological Phase

Thoughts and Feelings

Follow Up: Manifestation Date & Result

45

Notes

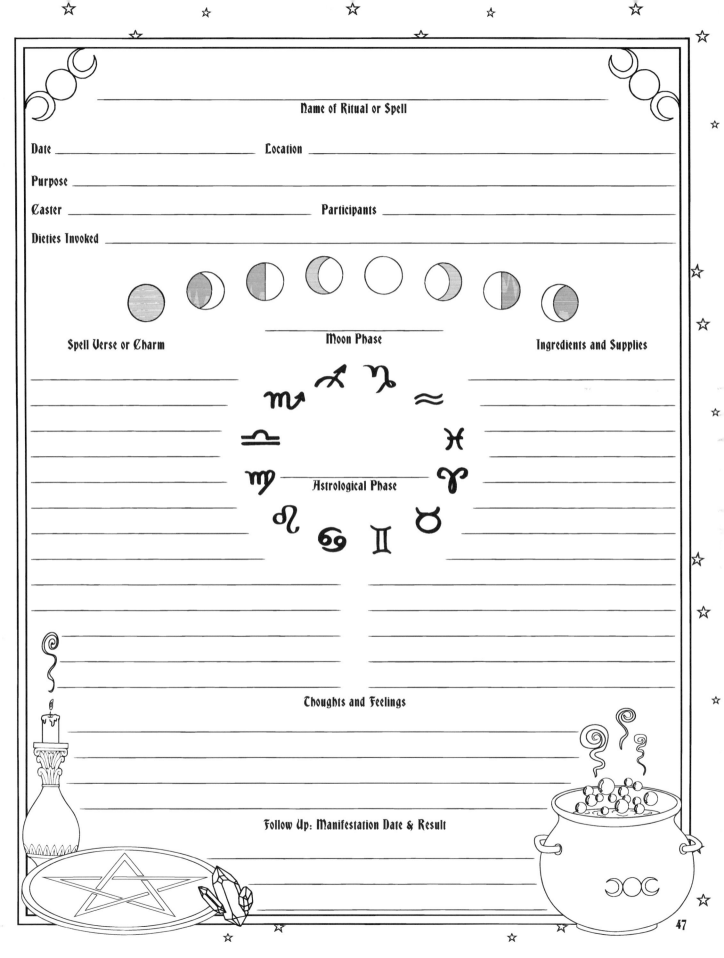

Name of Ritual or Spell

Date _____ Location _____

Purpose _____

Caster _____ Participants _____

Dieties Invoked _____

Spell Verse or Charm   **Moon Phase**   **Ingredients and Supplies**

Astrological Phase

Thoughts and Feelings

Follow Up: Manifestation Date & Result

Notes

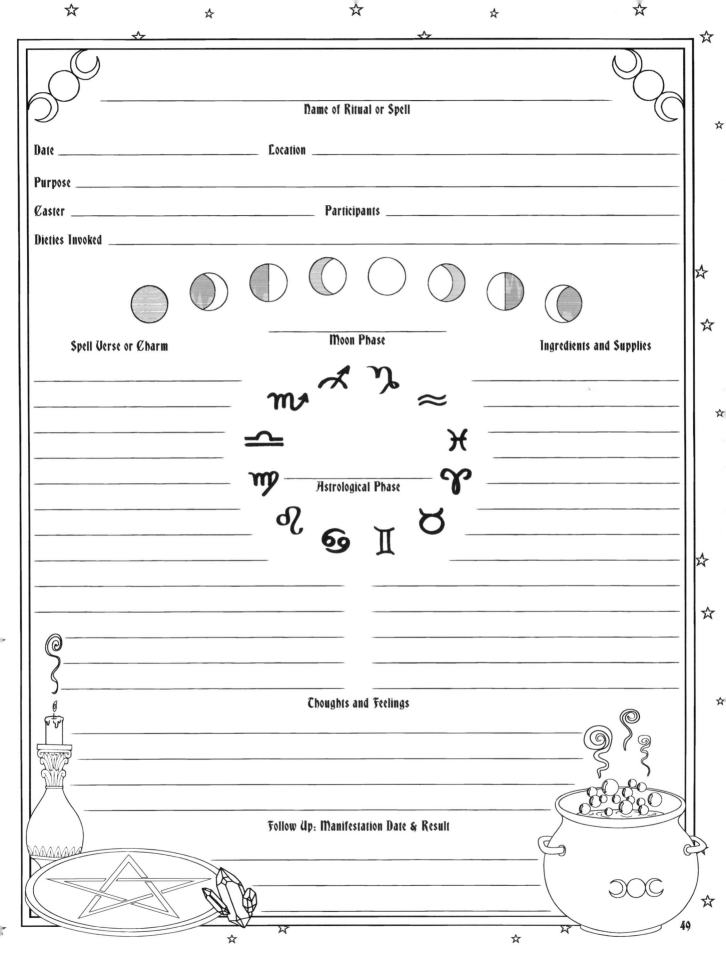

_____
Name of Ritual or Spell

Date _____ Location _____

Purpose _____

Caster _____ Participants _____

Dieties Invoked _____

Spell Verse or Charm   Moon Phase   Ingredients and Supplies

_____   _____
_____   Astrological Phase   _____
_____   _____
_____   _____
_____   _____
_____   _____
_____   _____
_____   _____
_____   _____

Thoughts and Feelings

_____
_____

Follow Up: Manifestation Date & Result

_____

49

Notes

_____

Name of Ritual or Spell

Date _____   Location _____

Purpose _____

Caster _____   Participants _____

Dieties Invoked _____

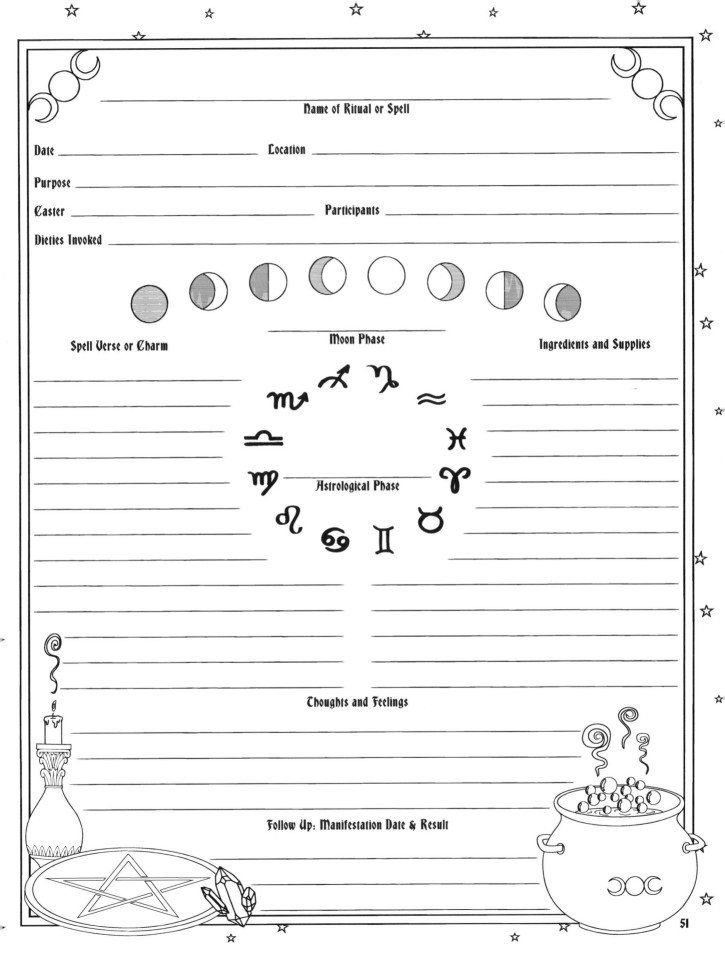

Spell Verse or Charm   **Moon Phase**   **Ingredients and Supplies**

Astrological Phase

Thoughts and Feelings

Follow Up: Manifestation Date & Result

Notes

_____

Name of Ritual or Spell

Date _____ Location _____

Purpose _____

Caster _____ Participants _____

Dieties Invoked _____

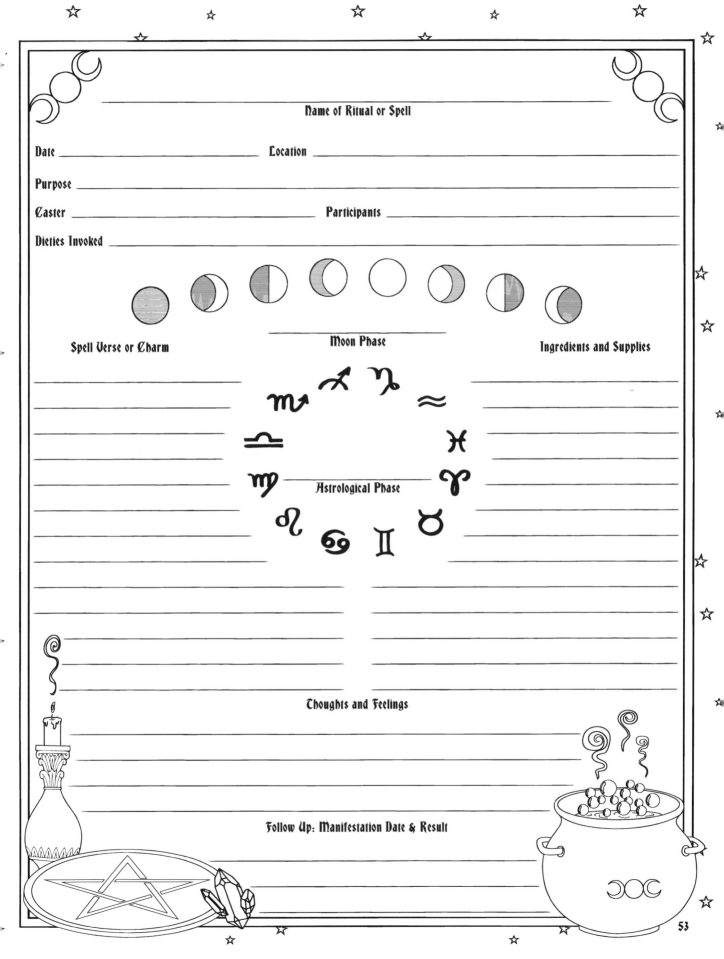

Spell Verse or Charm   **Moon Phase**   **Ingredients and Supplies**

Astrological Phase

Thoughts and Feelings

Follow Up: Manifestation Date & Result

Notes

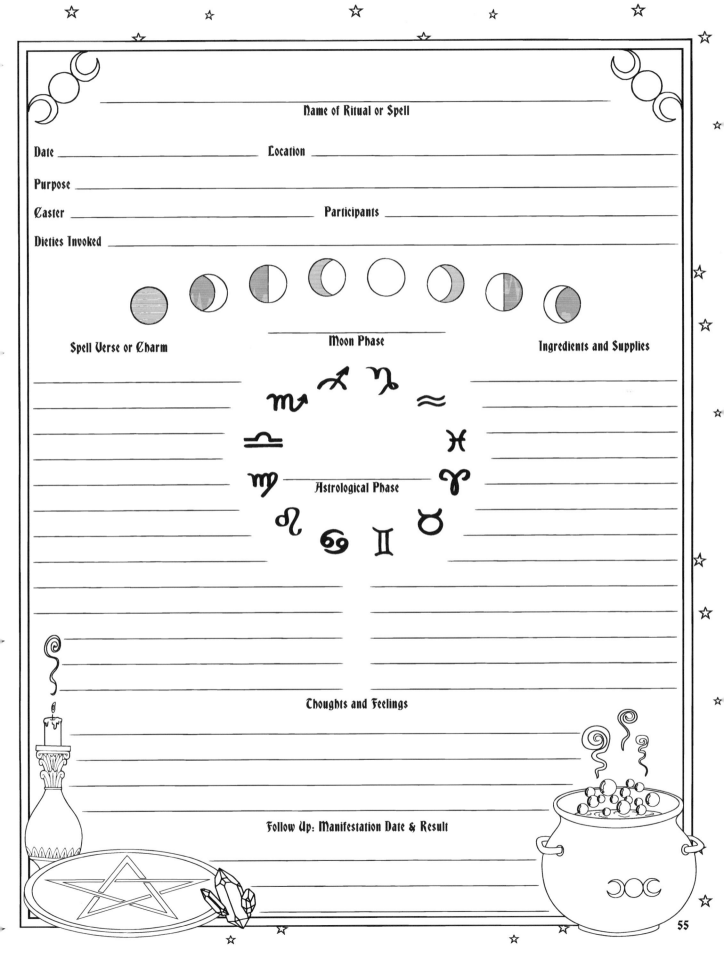

_____
Name of Ritual or Spell

Date _____   Location _____

Purpose _____

Caster _____   Participants _____

Dieties Invoked _____

Spell Verse or Charm   Moon Phase   Ingredients and Supplies

Astrological Phase

Thoughts and Feelings

Follow Up: Manifestation Date & Result

Notes

_____
Name of Ritual or Spell

Date _____ **Location** _____

Purpose _____

Caster _____ **Participants** _____

Dieties Invoked _____

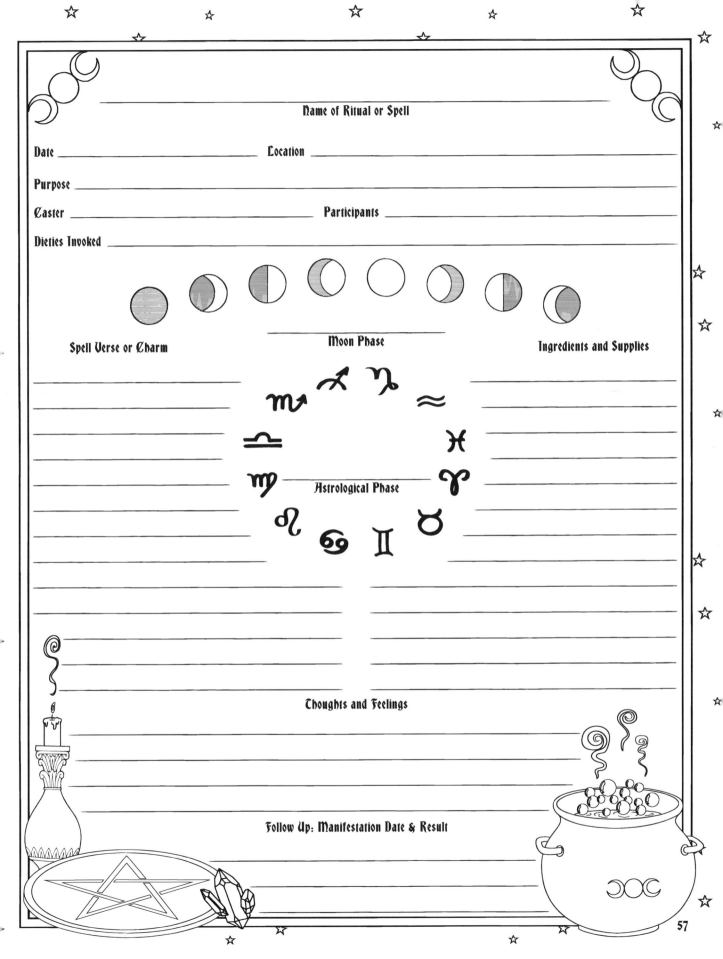

Spell Verse or Charm   **Moon Phase**   **Ingredients and Supplies**

Astrological Phase

Thoughts and Feelings

Follow Up: Manifestation Date & Result

Notes

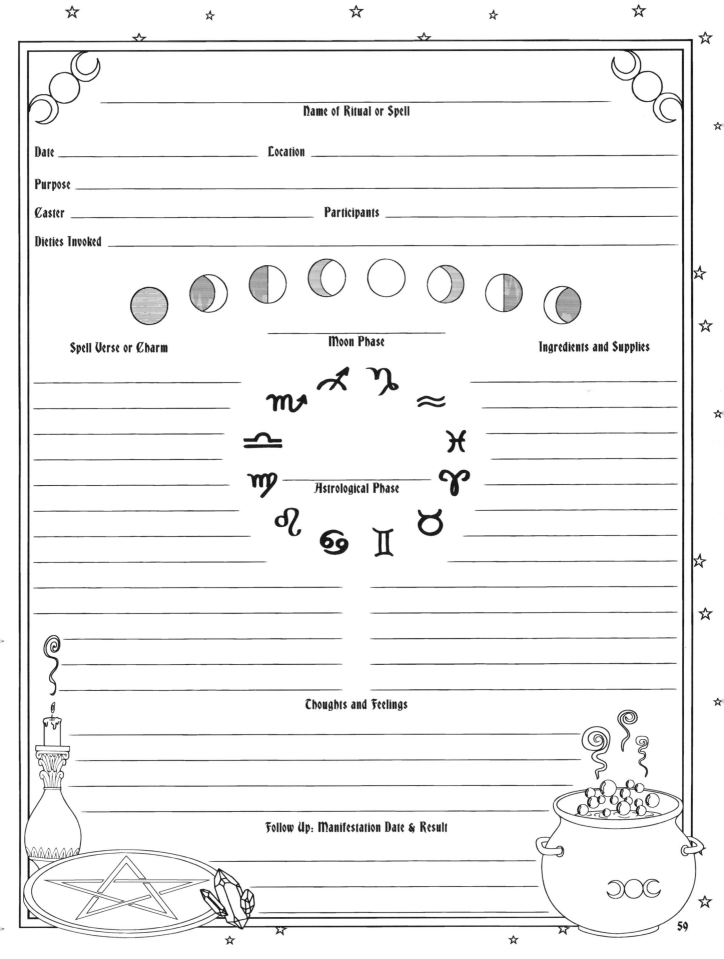

_____
Name of Ritual or Spell

Date _____ Location _____

Purpose _____

Caster _____ Participants _____

Dieties Invoked _____

Spell Verse or Charm   Moon Phase   Ingredients and Supplies

Astrological Phase

Thoughts and Feelings

Follow Up: Manifestation Date & Result

Notes

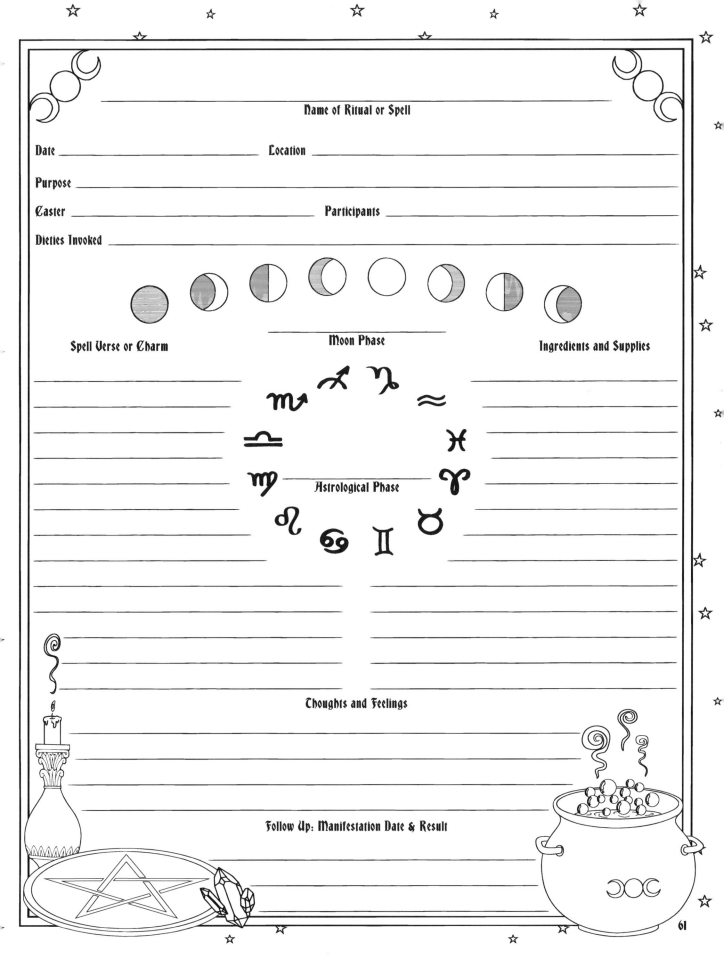

_____
Name of Ritual or Spell

Date _____   Location _____

Purpose _____

Caster _____   Participants _____

Dieties Invoked _____

Spell Verse or Charm   Moon Phase   Ingredients and Supplies

Astrological Phase

Thoughts and Feelings

Follow Up: Manifestation Date & Result

Notes

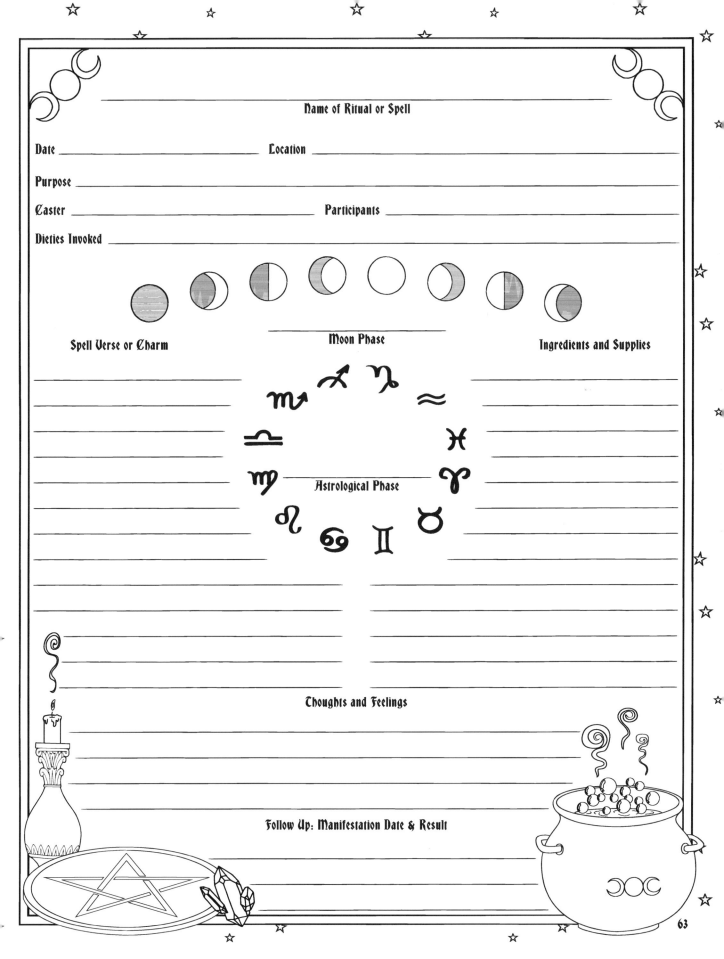

_____
Name of Ritual or Spell

Date _____ **Location** _____

Purpose _____

Caster _____ **Participants** _____

Dieties Invoked _____

Spell Verse or Charm   **Moon Phase**   **Ingredients and Supplies**

Astrological Phase

Thoughts and Feelings

Follow Up: Manifestation Date & Result

Notes

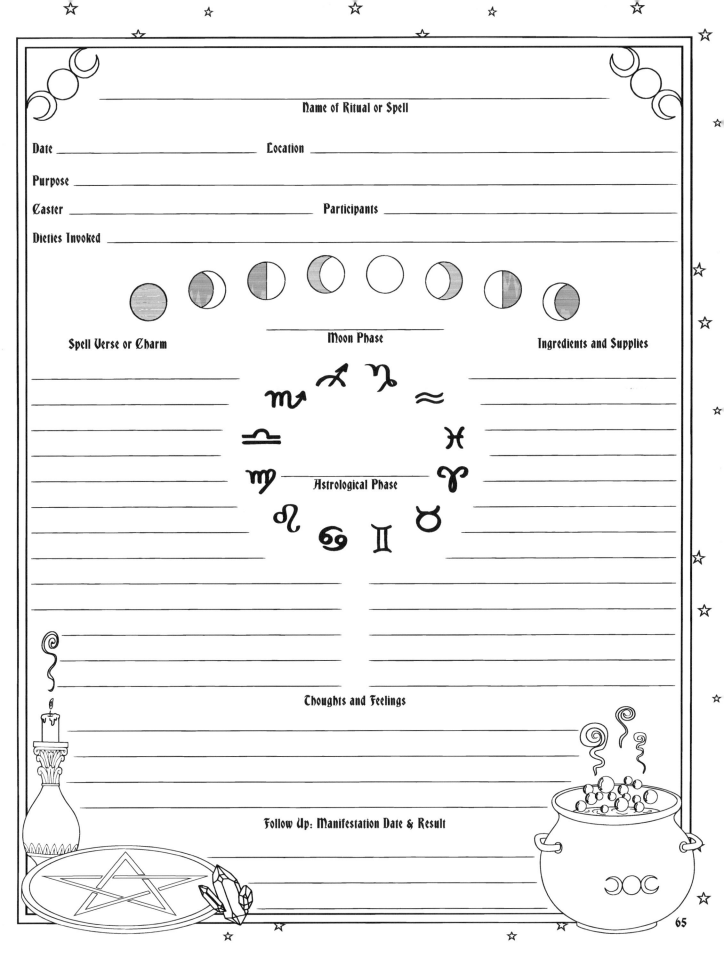

Name of Ritual or Spell

Date _____ Location _____

Purpose _____

Caster _____ Participants _____

Dieties Invoked _____

Spell Verse or Charm　　　　**Moon Phase**　　　　**Ingredients and Supplies**

Astrological Phase

Thoughts and Feelings

Follow Up: Manifestation Date & Result

Notes

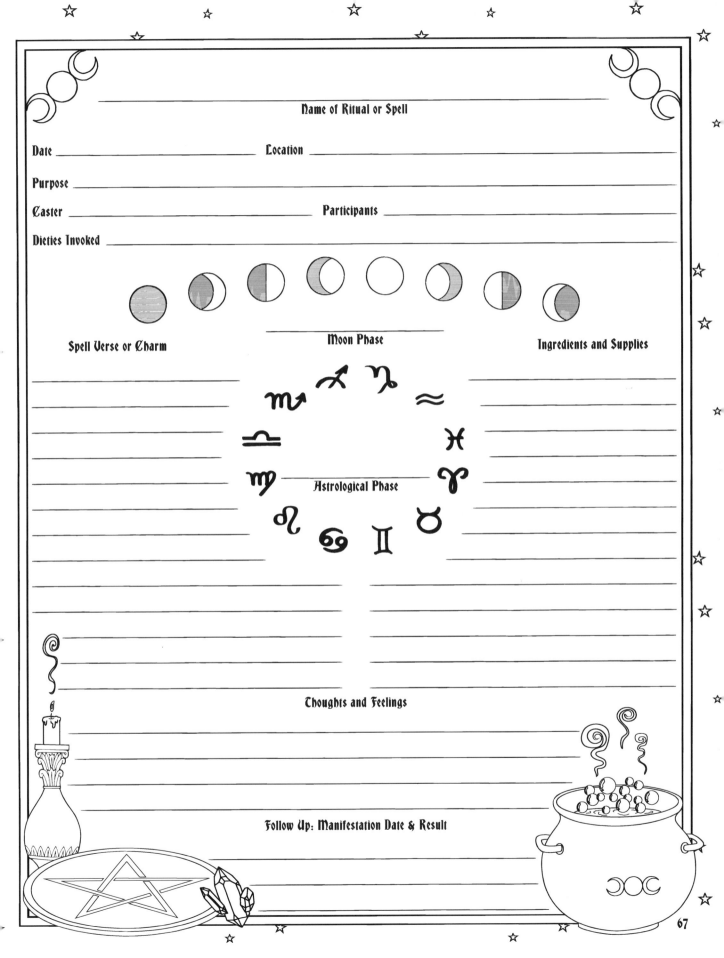

_____

Name of Ritual or Spell

Date _____ **Location** _____

Purpose _____

Caster _____ **Participants** _____

Dieties Invoked _____

Spell Verse or Charm **Moon Phase** **Ingredients and Supplies**

Astrological Phase

Thoughts and Feelings

Follow Up: Manifestation Date & Result

Notes

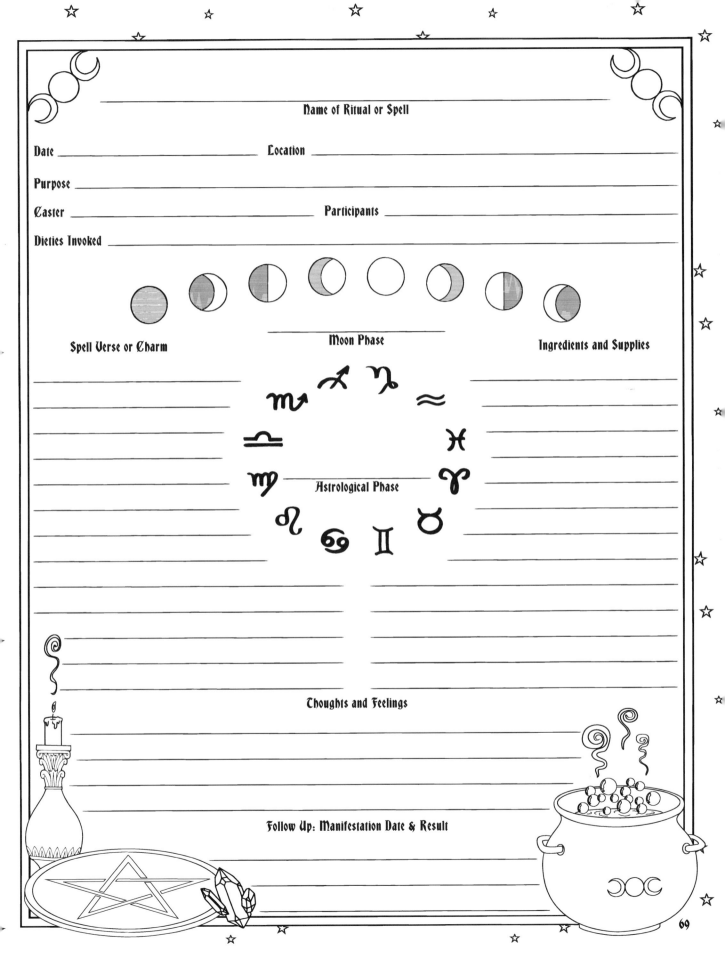

Name of Ritual or Spell

Date _____   Location _____

Purpose _____

Caster _____   Participants _____

Dieties Invoked _____

Spell Verse or Charm   Moon Phase   Ingredients and Supplies

Astrological Phase

Thoughts and Feelings

Follow Up: Manifestation Date & Result

Notes

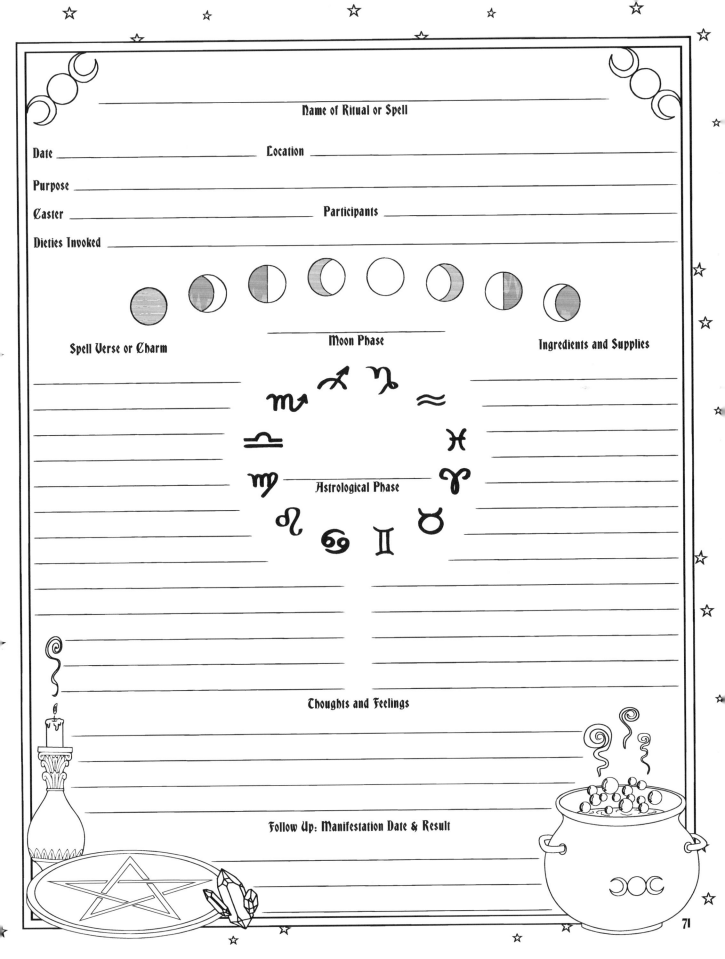

Name of Ritual or Spell

Date _____ Location _____

Purpose _____

Caster _____ Participants _____

Dieties Invoked _____

Spell Verse or Charm   Moon Phase   Ingredients and Supplies

Astrological Phase

Thoughts and Feelings

Follow Up: Manifestation Date & Result

Notes

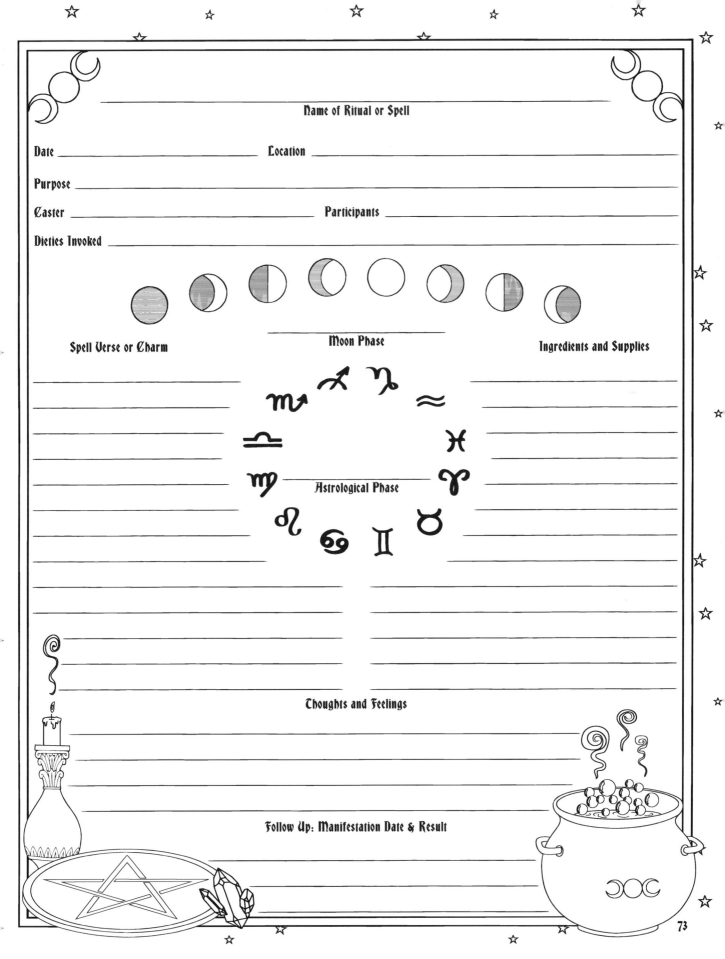

_____
Name of Ritual or Spell

Date _____ Location _____

Purpose _____

Caster _____ Participants _____

Dieties Invoked _____

Spell Verse or Charm   Moon Phase   Ingredients and Supplies

Astrological Phase

Thoughts and Feelings

Follow Up: Manifestation Date & Result

Notes

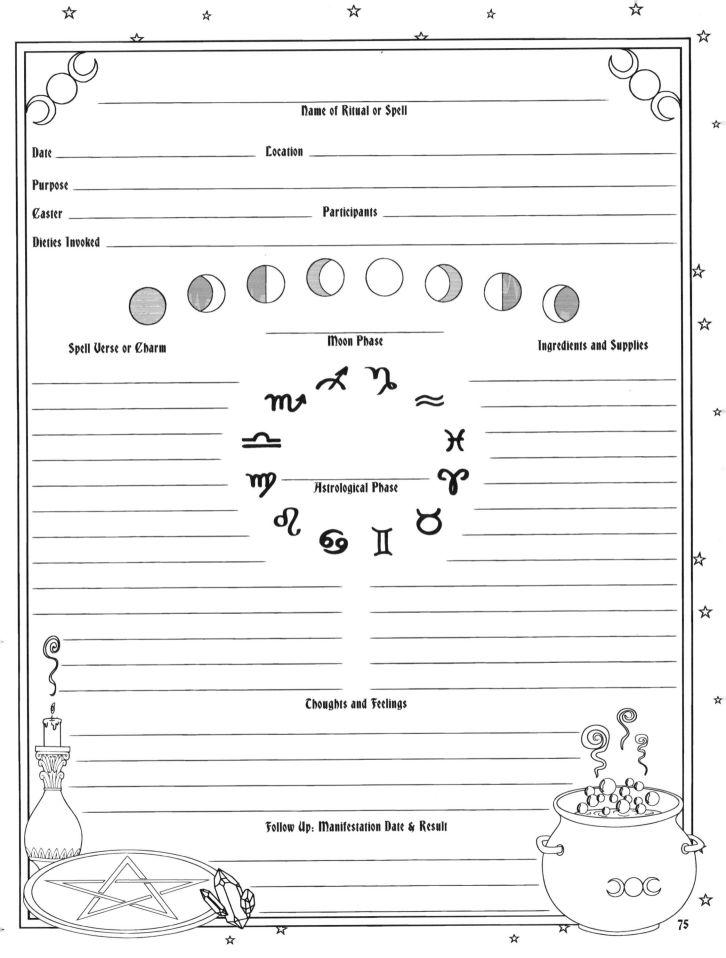

_____
Name of Ritual or Spell

Date _____ Location _____

Purpose _____

Caster _____ Participants _____

Dieties Invoked _____

Spell Verse or Charm   **Moon Phase**   **Ingredients and Supplies**

_____   **Astrological Phase**   _____
_____   _____
_____   _____
_____   _____
_____   _____
_____   _____
_____   _____
_____   _____
_____   _____

Thoughts and Feelings

_____
_____
_____

Follow Up: Manifestation Date & Result

_____
_____

Notes

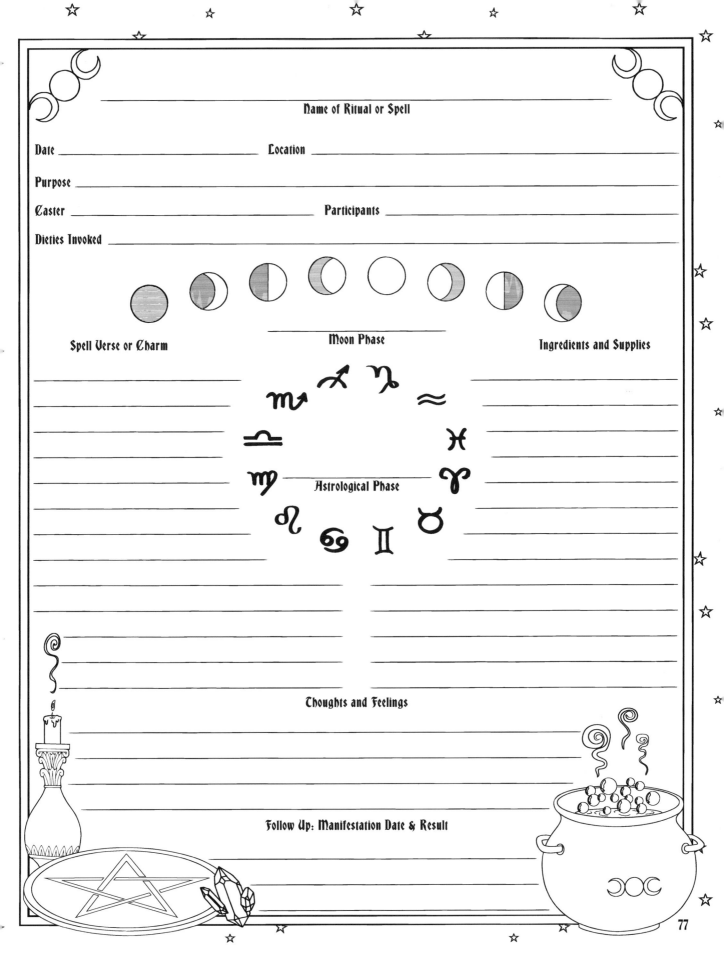

_____
Name of Ritual or Spell

Date _____ Location _____

Purpose _____

Caster _____ Participants _____

Dieties Invoked _____

Spell Verse or Charm   Moon Phase   Ingredients and Supplies

Astrological Phase

Thoughts and Feelings

Follow Up: Manifestation Date & Result

Notes

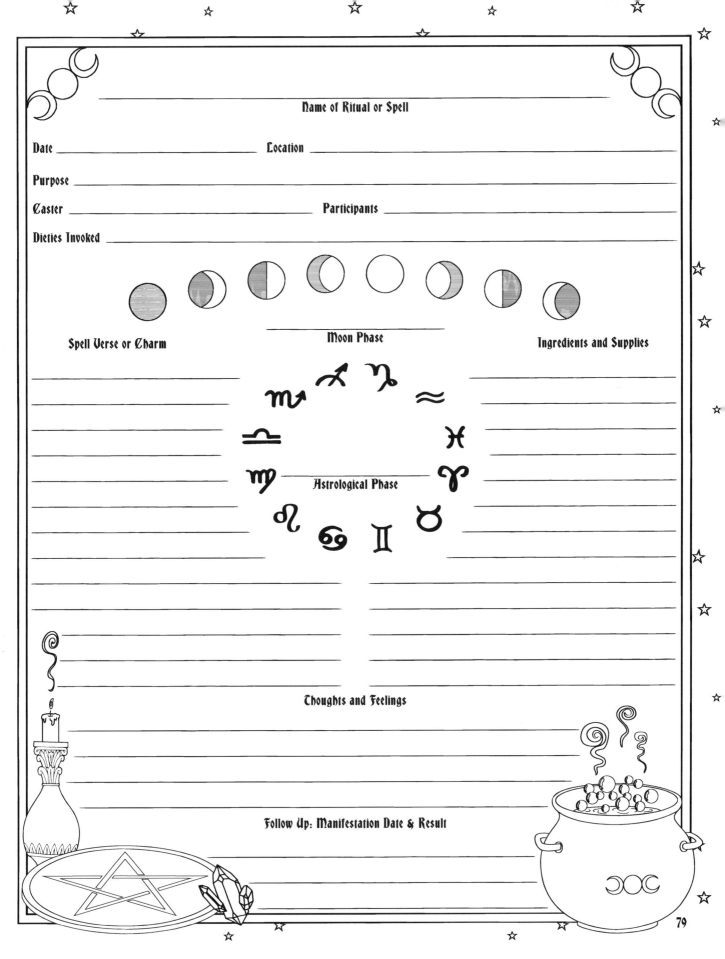

Name of Ritual or Spell

Date _____ Location _____

Purpose _____

Caster _____ Participants _____

Dieties Invoked _____

Spell Verse or Charm   Moon Phase   Ingredients and Supplies

Astrological Phase

Thoughts and Feelings

Follow Up: Manifestation Date & Result

Notes

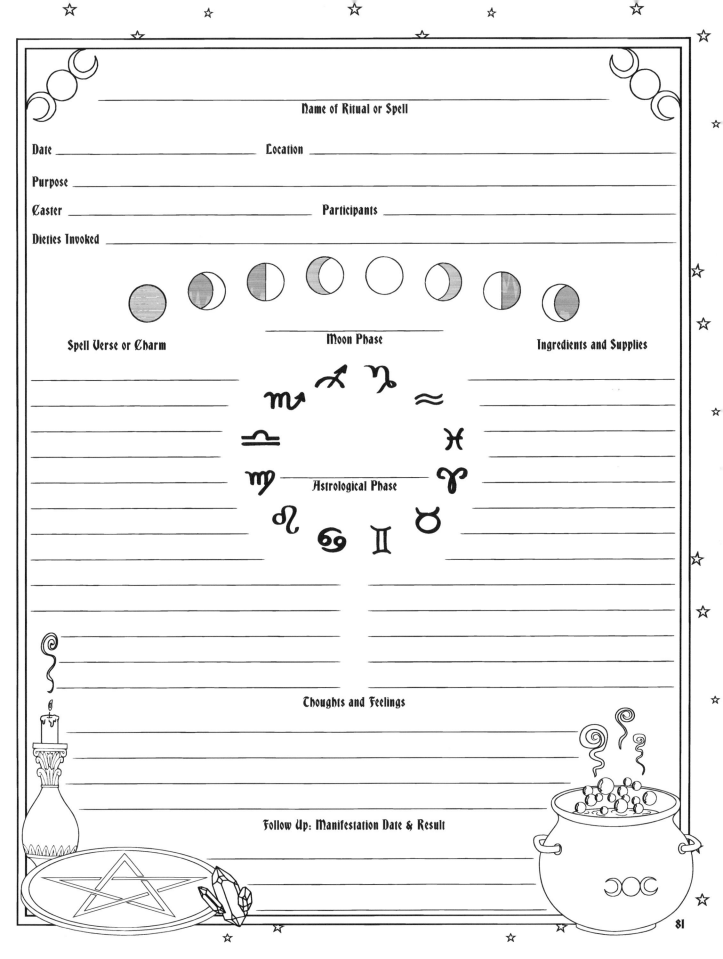

Name of Ritual or Spell

Date _____   **Location** _____

Purpose _____

Caster _____   **Participants** _____

Dieties Invoked _____

Spell Verse or Charm   **Moon Phase**   **Ingredients and Supplies**

Astrological Phase

Thoughts and Feelings

Follow Up: Manifestation Date & Result

81

Notes

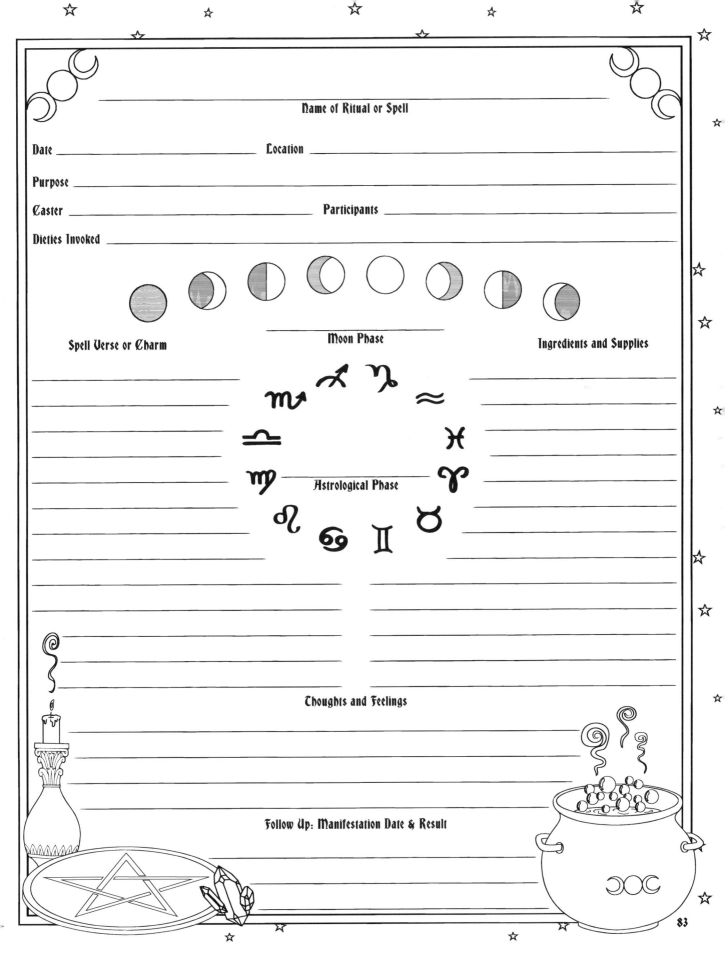

Name of Ritual or Spell

Date _____ Location _____

Purpose _____

Caster _____ Participants _____

Dieties Invoked _____

Spell Verse or Charm   Moon Phase   Ingredients and Supplies

Astrological Phase

Thoughts and Feelings

Follow Up: Manifestation Date & Result

Notes

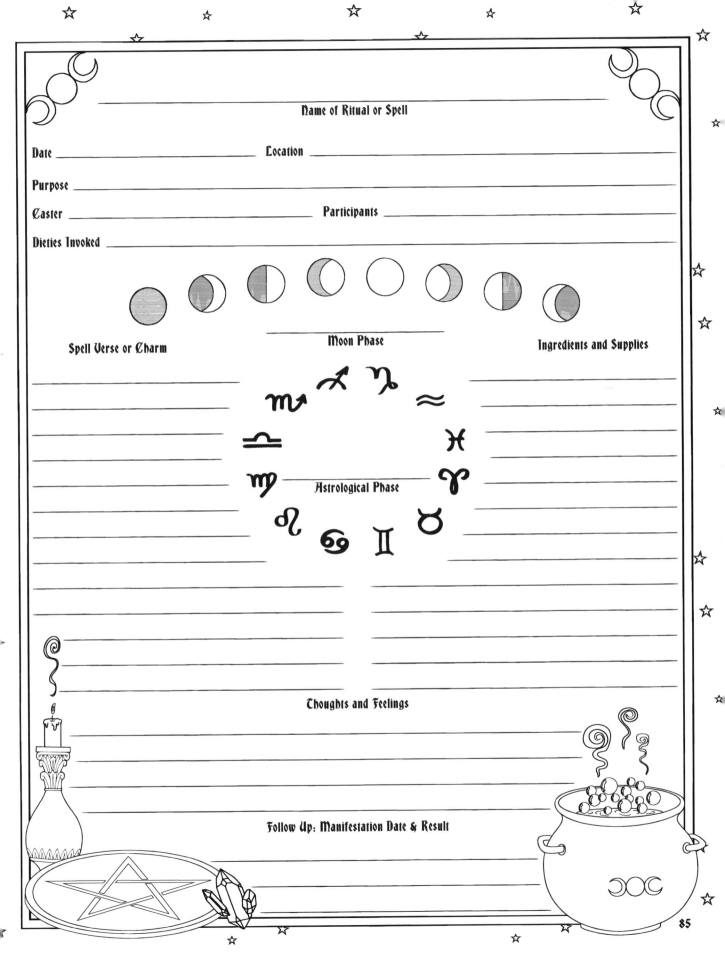

_____ Name of Ritual or Spell

Date _____ Location _____

Purpose _____

Caster _____ Participants _____

Dieties Invoked _____

Spell Verse or Charm   Moon Phase   Ingredients and Supplies

Astrological Phase

Thoughts and Feelings

Follow Up: Manifestation Date & Result

85

Notes

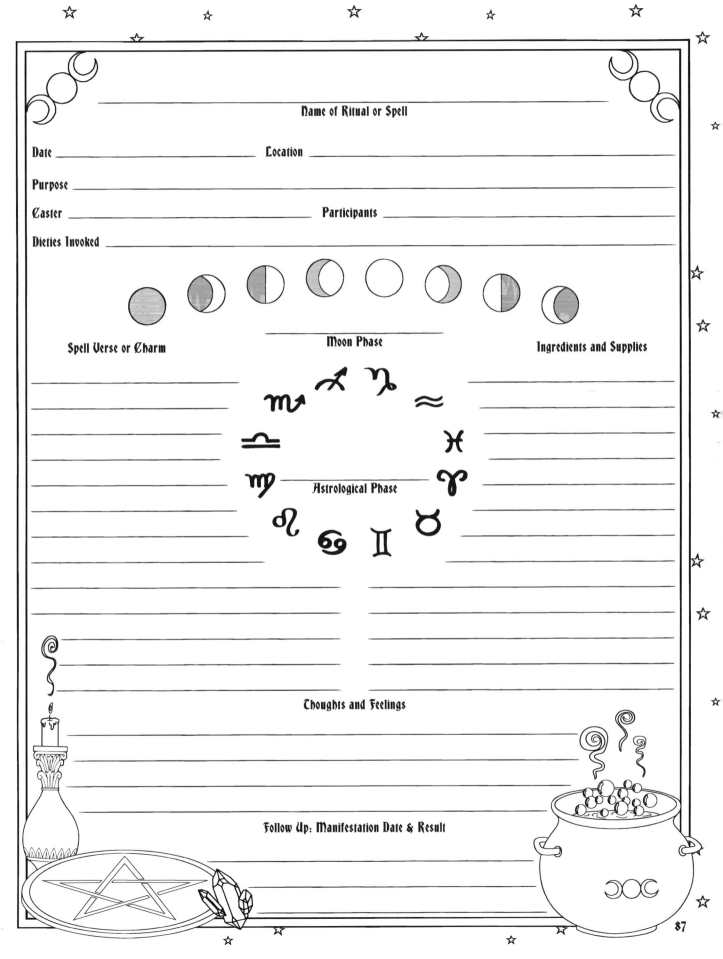

_____
Name of Ritual or Spell

Date _____   Location _____

Purpose _____

Caster _____   Participants _____

Dieties Invoked _____

Spell Verse or Charm   Moon Phase   Ingredients and Supplies

_____   _____
_____   Astrological Phase   _____
_____   _____
_____   _____
_____   _____
_____   _____
_____   _____
_____   _____
_____   _____
_____   _____

Thoughts and Feelings

_____
_____
_____

Follow Up: Manifestation Date & Result

_____
_____

87

Notes

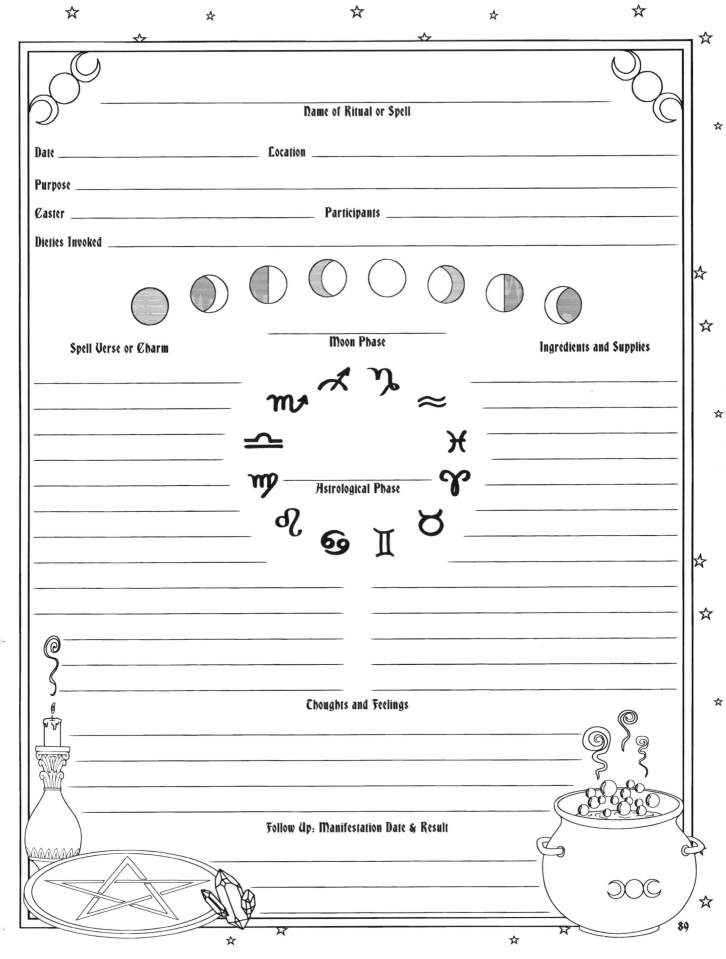

_____
Name of Ritual or Spell

Date _____ **Location** _____

Purpose _____

Caster _____ **Participants** _____

Dieties Invoked _____

Spell Verse or Charm　　　　**Moon Phase**　　　　**Ingredients and Supplies**

Astrological Phase

Thoughts and Feelings

Follow Up: Manifestation Date & Result

Notes

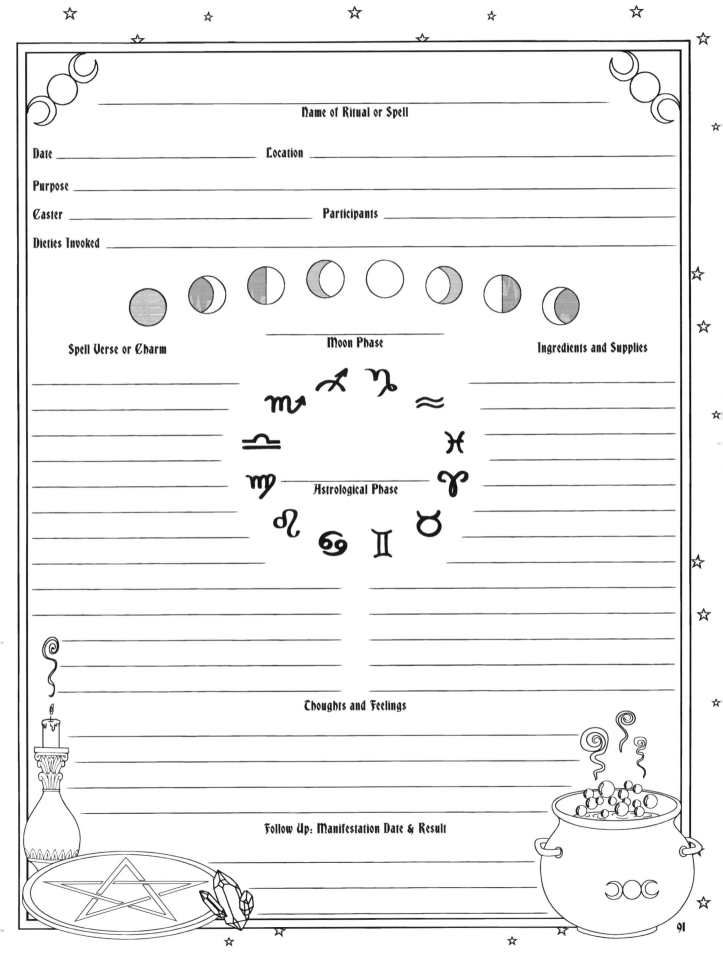

_____
Name of Ritual or Spell

Date _____   Location _____

Purpose _____

Caster _____   Participants _____

Dieties Invoked _____

Spell Verse or Charm   Moon Phase   Ingredients and Supplies

Astrological Phase

Thoughts and Feelings

Follow Up: Manifestation Date & Result

Notes

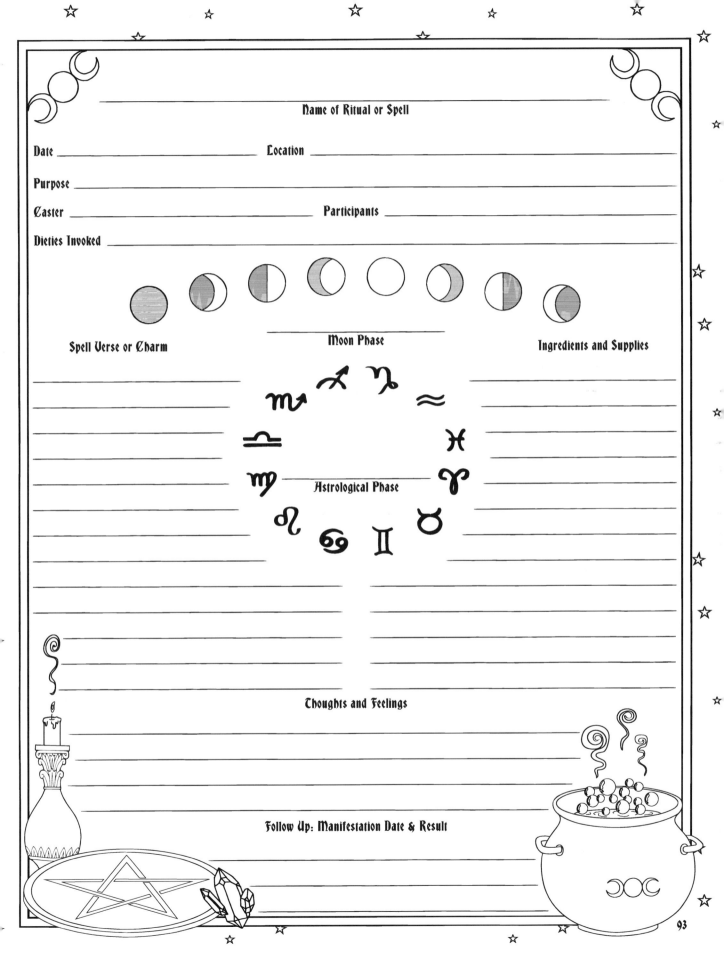

_____ **Name of Ritual or Spell**

Date _____ **Location** _____

Purpose _____

Caster _____ **Participants** _____

Dieties Invoked _____

Spell Verse or Charm   **Moon Phase**   **Ingredients and Supplies**

Astrological Phase

Thoughts and Feelings

Follow Up: Manifestation Date & Result

Notes

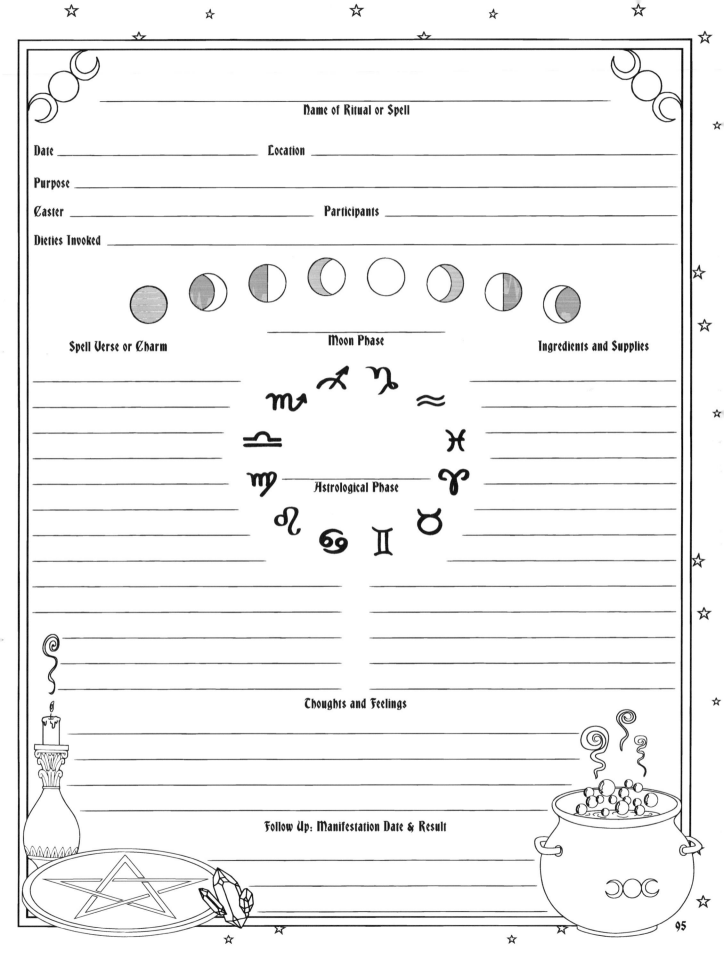

_____
Name of Ritual or Spell

Date _____ Location _____

Purpose _____

Caster _____ Participants _____

Dieties Invoked _____

Spell Verse or Charm   Moon Phase   Ingredients and Supplies

_____   _____   _____
_____   _____   _____
_____   _____   _____
_____   Astrological Phase   _____
_____   _____
_____   _____
_____   _____
_____   _____
_____
_____

Thoughts and Feelings

_____
_____
_____
_____

Follow Up: Manifestation Date & Result

_____
_____

Notes

_____
Name of Ritual or Spell

Date _____ **Location** _____

Purpose _____

Caster _____ **Participants** _____

Dieties Invoked _____

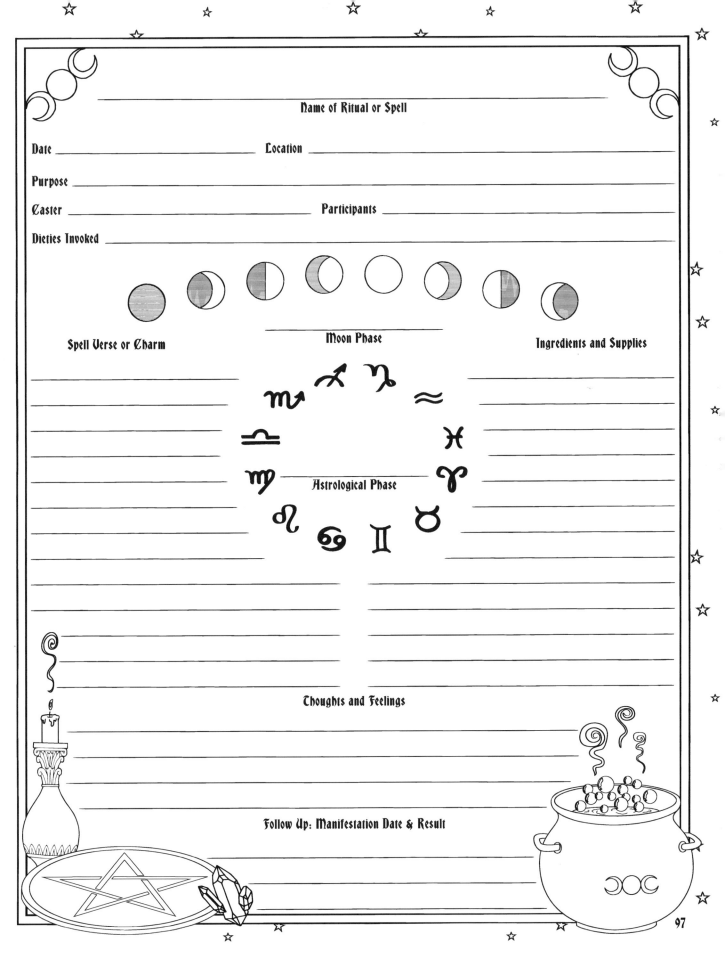

Spell Verse or Charm   **Moon Phase**   **Ingredients and Supplies**

Astrological Phase

Thoughts and Feelings

Follow Up: Manifestation Date & Result

Notes

Notes

Notes

Notes

Notes

Notes

Notes

Notes

Notes

Notes

Made in the USA
Las Vegas, NV
28 June 2024

91632338R00072